"This guide shows how to get beyond the shoc prices, showcasing selective (richer) colleges aid policies... as well as funding for paid summ away terms... and big career networks, all of w underdog students."

> — Dr. Lisa Brandes, Asst. Dean for Student Affairs,
> Yale Graduate School of Arts and Sciences (retired)

"Many high school students think the cost of a college education makes it an unattainable goal. Abi takes a daunting and stressful process and breaks it down into doable and manageable steps. A joy to read..."

> — Beth Chancy, Sr. Associate Director, Career Services,
> University of Richmond

"...A beacon of hope and practical wisdom. Abi has crafted a comprehensive roadmap...but also empowers all students to navigate their academic journey with resilience and purpose."

> — Karim Abouelnaga, Author of Breaking Through From Rough to
> Ready and The Purpose-Driven Social Entrepreneur

"A step-by-step practical guide for winning scholarships... Abi Olvera shares her own story of a first-gen Latina in an honest and engaging manner... Also a must-read for high school counselors and college admission officers!"

> — George Hiller, 2016 Adjust Instructor of the Year,
> Robins School of Business, University of Richmond

"...An invaluable resource for students from low-income backgrounds... Abi seamlessly weaves her personal story with concrete, tactical advice on becoming the type of student universities fight over."

> — Anemone Franz, Advisor, 80,000 Hours

"WOW! If we all had this when we were pursuing higher education, we would have experienced less stress and had our education financed."

> — Arvis Jones, Director, Student Leadership & Campus Life,
> El Paso Community College (retired)

"...An incredibly practical guide...full of concrete specific examples and steps to aid students as they pursue their dream."

> — Caryl McFarlane, Strategy Consultant, Former Senior Program
> Officer at Woodrow Wilson National Fellowship Foundation

To the University of Richmond, and all the generous institutions across the country offering guaranteed aid to students from disadvantaged backgrounds - this is for you and the students you empower.

To El Paso Community College because, as your slogan goes, you really were "the best place to start!"

To the mentors, teachers, and scholarship donors who believed in, invested in, and supported me throughout my journey - without you, I would have never learned what I'm capable of.

To my brother, who showed me that opportunity must be seized, not waited for.

To my dad, whose belief in me never wavered, even when the path did.

And to all the students who feel stuck or don't yet see a path forward - there is light ahead.

This book is dedicated to igniting that spark of hope.

THE UNDERDOG'S GUIDE TO
SCHOLARSHIPS

BY ABI OLVERA

CONTENTS

CHAPTER 1

HOW TO GET NEARLY FULL SCHOLARSHIPS

WIN REGARDLESS OF WHETHER
YOU'RE IN HIGH SCHOOL OR COLLEGE

Are you confused by the process of getting into a good college and paying for it? Are you the first in your family to try to do this? Does your family, like 42 percent of Americans, have *no more than $1,000 in savings*, making it impossible (or at least nonsensical), factoring in your current minimum-wage job, to take out $40,000+ in loans to pay for a degree, especially without a guarantee of a job that will earn you enough to pay them back? Do you happen not to be in the top 10 percent of your class as it is, making the idea of getting into any school, let alone a top-tier school, incredibly daunting?

If you can reply "yes" to *any* of these questions, this book is for you, and here's why: as a high school senior, I could reply "yes" to *all* of them.

I wanted to go to college, and I was completely and utterly bewildered. Out-of-state universities cost $40,000 to $75,000 per year, and local public universities cost "only" $7,000 to $12,000. My family lacked savings and know-how on college scholarships. My mother worked inconsistent jobs that paid low wages. My father had inconsistent income from his construction company. I had been working minimum wage jobs since I was fifteen. Even if I worked full-time after high school, my earnings as a server would not be enough to afford public university. I groveled to my local university's scholarship office. They couldn't do anything since I didn't qualify to so much as *apply* for the university's merit-based scholarships because I wasn't in the top 10 percent of my high school. I spent my last semesters of high school desperately applying for scholarships, winning none.

Perhaps you're like me: college wasn't always the obvious next step. Unlike some students who had family legacies or expectations around higher ed, my path felt unclear. I just knew I wanted more for my future than my parents had. I wanted financial security, impactful career opportunities, and the chance to explore the world. College seemed like the way to make those dreams happen, even if I didn't totally understand how yet.

The stats made college a clear choice, too - a degree doubles your odds of employment and nets over a million more dollars[1] over your lifetime.

So I decided to take a risk and invest in myself. I made it my goal to attend university. In order to do this I had to see *myself* as the start-up that I was founding..

After hours of googling universities, I realized that many universities' tuition and board costs were more than what my family was making. So much for getting to experience dorm life and exploring a new city. I didn't even bother asking my parents if we could afford these—most of their earnings went to housing and car repairs.

Flailing, underinformed, I picked the local university, which broke up the tuition and fees into an installment plan of small payments throughout the semester. I talked my father into taking turns with me on the payments.

In no time I felt like a mouse on a hamster wheel, struggling to get enough hours at my multiple jobs to keep up with payments, while also putting in the time to be an excellent student. I read online that to be considered a "**top student**" for scholarships, one needed extracurriculars as well as grades (both of which are essential to growth and success, something I discuss later).

I realized I had no chance of getting scholarships unless I found time to be a top student, and that without enough money, I was drowning trying to earn enough to pay tuition. I transferred to a community college, where tuition and fees were low enough to be covered by my *automatic* government grant (the **Pell Grant**), freeing up my time to dive deep into extracurriculars.

Throughout those next three semesters at community college, I optimized my day-to-day to turn myself into the exact

---

1   https://www.aplu.org/our-work/4-policy-and-advocacy/publicuvalues/employment-earnings

kind of student that got big scholarships. I ended up receiving about $150,000 in scholarships for undergrad alone. (In my senior year, I was offered *two* $50,000+ scholarships at the same time. The extra money above the cost of university didn't go to me, unfortunately.) What I did in those three semesters also helped me win a national fellowship in my junior year that paid for my master's degree and boosted my résumé enough to get me into a school I thought I was crazy to even dream about: Yale. That national fellowship also landed me two paid internships: one in Washington, D.C., and one abroad. After my master's, I went on to become a U.S. diplomat, serving in Senegal, Egypt, and Washington, D.C.

Back then, I couldn't see how rare I was: a low-income student aiming for top universities, where the average student's family income was over $200,000. My economic status actually helped me. I qualified for *automatic* scholarships, *guaranteed* entirely due to the rarity of being a low-income student accepted at those specific universities. A common word for people like me—and, perhaps, like you—is "disadvantaged." The word that I came to realize is more applicable is *"unicorn."*

This book is a step-by-step breakdown of what I did to get those big automatic scholarships, and later that fellowship... and how you can do it too. You can start this journey regardless of what year of high school you're in, and even as a college freshman.

Select chapters will be helpful to students of all incomes, but students coming from families making less than $70,000 will derive the greatest benefit from this book. In these chapters, I'll show you why it makes financial sense for you to target top (rich) schools, and then I'll tell you how you can set yourself up to get into them, as someone who has been through this process firsthand.

If your family makes significantly over $70,000 a year or has significant assets, this book's university selection strategies don't apply to you, but you may find useful the list of schools that offer no-loans financial aid packages to students of *all* in-comes (see Chapter 2). Applicable to everyone are my strate-gies for getting great grades, picking unique extracurriculars, and assembling a team of mentors (Chapters 4, 5, and 6).

Most of this book will help students in any year of high school get into a university that covers their **full financial need**, from the jump. Some parts are specifically geared for high school seniors about to start at public colleges or for cur-rent college students, with the aim to help them transfer to those same top universities that will cover their needs. While it's more difficult to get into these generous universities as a transfer student, it is very much possible. I wrote the book in this way to underscore that it's not too late for you, even if—like me—you weren't competitive enough to get into these generous universities right out of high school.

In general, the top schools in America, those who also tend to charge $60,000+ a year, struggle to attract students from the lowest 50 percent of U.S. households by income. Universi-ties have long been scrutinized for how much income diversi-ty they have; hence, universities started offering financial aid guarantees, or *automatic scholarships.*

You probably haven't heard of these financial aid guarantees because most college strategy information is geared toward students whose families make well over $70,000. The average student's family income at private colleges is around $91,000. And at selective schools it's much higher - think $272,000 at Washington University in St. Louis, and $244,000 at Middle-bury College in Vermont. The situation is so lopsided that the *New York Times* even found that thirty-eight U.S. colleges ac-cepted more students from the top 1 percent than the bottom 60 percent of U.S. families by income[2]

The extreme college inequality can be a blessing in disguise. These universities need less affluent students like us to bal-ance out their student body. And the universities have the cash

2   https://www.nytimes.com/interactive/projects/college-mobility.

to pay for us since wealthy families drop $60,000+ a year on tuition.

This is also why schools with great aid often have incredible amenities too. The university I chose, University of Richmond offered a free study abroad semester - I spent a summer in Switzerland without spending a dime. The university even gave us $1,000 just for lunch money, which I stretched into backpacking through Europe.

Back on campus, I got $4000 per semester in "dining dollars" for smoothies, lattes, snacks - anything I wanted from the stores, restaurants, and cafes on campus. For the first time in my life, I stocked up on fancy protein bars and ordered appetizers without worrying about price. There was even a free Dance Dance Revolution arcade machine in the university gym near my dorm.

Going to a top-tier school with automatic scholarships was the best decision I ever made.

Quick Summary of the College Financial Aid System:

Types of financial aid awards offered by universities to admitted students:

Need-based scholarships *are given to students based on financial need. Recipients have been accepted to the university, and the university uses these scholarships to make education affordable for them.*

Merit-based scholarships *are given to students based on their academic, artistic, athletic, or other achievements. Recipients have been accepted to the university, and the university aims to entice the student to choose this university over another university by offering a competitive scholarship package.*

Automatic scholarships *are awards that are given to students who meet certain criteria, such as grade point average (GPA), class rank, or test scores. This book discusses, primarily, automatic scholarships that are disbursed on the bases of two criteria: (1) acceptance to a university; and (2) student's family income or demonstrated need.*

Other financial-aid sources, not from universities:
Private scholarships *are awards given by various organizations, companies, or individuals to provide financial aid to students who meet specific criteria. Large private scholarships ($20,000+) are very difficult to get.*

COLLEGE TUITION PRICES ARE A LIE

The prices you see on colleges' websites are only accurate for families with incomes in the top 10 percent (over $200,000 a year). Not only do many universities give generous financial aid, but a growing number of universities also *guarantee* nearly full rides to students under a certain income. For families who make less than that (the level varies by university), *many universities promise to "meet all financial need."* If your family's income and assets mean they can only give $3,000 toward university expenses, then that's all that they would pay up front.

The "real" price of each university depends on *your income*. In general, the lower your income, the longer the list of schools that offer your income level an automatic scholarship. Thus, if you are a student with a family income below the **US.. median income** (*roughly $70,000*) and you simply get *admitted* to one of these universities, you'll get an automatic full or nearly full ride scholarship. No more having to worry about how to pay for university, racking up tons of debt, or even worrying about paying for rent or food, since these universities typically include dorm costs and meal plans in their scholarship awards.

A few top schools even give these automatic scholarships to students with high family incomes. For example, Princeton covers all tuition, room, and board for families with incomes up to $100,000. This is both a testament to how much more money expensive universities can spend toward financial aid *and* to just how few students from lower-income levels apply and get in.

It's not only super-selective colleges that offer automatic scholarships. The public university in my hometown, University of Texas at El Paso, now offers a similar promise to families making up to $75,000, though room and board are not included.

With these financial aid guarantees, top schools costing over $55,000 wound up cheaper than my local public university.

This strategy got me a pretty much full ride to the University of Richmond (which cost $55,000+ a year), including room and board.

WHERE THE MONEY REALLY IS

When people talk about scholarships, they tend to think of big-name private scholarships like the Coca-Cola Scholarship or other scholarships that are not tied to any school. These scholarships, however, are *very* hard to get—only a handful of students in the country receive these. Everyone's heard of them, so you'd be competing with thousands of students across the country.

Private scholarships like these are not how most students get money for college. *Selective universities end up giving 40 percent to 60 percent of admitted students financial aid packages using the university's financial aid funds.* The amount of aid can differ wildly because it depends on the school's generosity, how badly the university wants that specific student to attend, etc. Students usually apply to several universities to compare different and often very unpredictable financial aid offerings.

However, you are a unicorn because of your family income. Since your family income is less than the median family income in the United States, your scholarship offers will be much more predictable if you focus on schools that promise to meet full financial need. Because of these income-based automatic scholarships (also called "promises" or "guarantees"), you won't waste time applying to schools that will admit you but not shower you with money.

For you, the main concern is getting into one of these seventy-five or so universities.

BREAK AWAY FROM SOCIETAL EXPECTATIONS: EXPLORING YOUR POTENTIAL

Getting into a selective university might seem like an impossible feat. It's not. If you were in different social circles, getting into a selective university might have been your default step after high school.

After college, I crossed paths with Harvey, who attended an Ivy League university right after high school. He had followed a predetermined "norm" set by his social circle, where attending a selective university and pursuing a professional career was the default. These societal pressures meant he was expected to develop his skills (in music, for example), apply for prestigious summer camps, and join extracurriculars. This was the path most people around him took.

Reflecting on my own experience, I realized that my norms were limiting me. I didn't personally know many people who went to selective universities or had white-collar careers, so pursuing one myself was venturing into unfamiliar territory without a map. I thought that selective universities and cool careers like journalism, news anchoring, or writing were for other people. But as I gained more experience, I realized the people who went to these schools and got exciting careers were very real, very normal people who have also dropped their phone on their face while lying down, like I have.

So, take a moment to consider and challenge your own assumptions and beliefs.

- What assumptions have you made about what is possible for you?

- What do your family and friends expect of you? What do they expect of themselves?

- Do you come from a place where hourly wages are the norm, and the idea of a so-called professional career seems like a distant dream?

- If your parents were in your dream profession, would that path, then, seem more achievable?

- Based on the people around you, your family, and your friends, where do you expect to go after high school?

- How would your life be different if you had seen those around you pursue their dream careers?

- What would excite you to achieve and do?

- Does your ideal life seem achievable?

- Do you believe that in the future you will be stuck, scraping by, or will you have options and be living the life you've always dreamed of?

Now, imagine if everyone around you had gotten great grades and went to selective universities, because that's what everyone around them does. You likely wouldn't question your ability to do the same!

This book provides a step-by-step process to excel in college, but you also need to discard, consciously, any limiting beliefs about how far you can go.

If you've ever been on free or reduced-price lunch at school, wondered who the people are who can afford to go on far-away family vacations, hoped for name-brand shoes rather than the knock-offs, stressed about the price of the school field trips, extracurriculars, and yearbooks, or been expected to get a job at a young age, this book is for you. You are unique for committing yourself to top universities, where the family income of students is typically $200,000+. By committing yourself to your goals and working hard, you can get scholarships to the top schools that will launch your career.

On this journey, you'll learn a lot about how capable you are of accomplishing things you may not have considered. The people who have achieved your dreams are probably not that much different from you. They still feel awkward at parties, clumsily practice guitar for hours to progress, and need to keep track of deadlines to not forget. The biggest difference is that these people are more confident in themselves and have a track record that helped them build momentum. I never saw myself as someone who could write a book, become a diplomat, or start a youth empowerment hub. That all changed when I met people who I could identify with, but who were doing these incredible things.

GETTING INTO GENEROUS SELECTIVE COLLEGES: EXPLAINED

Getting into one of these generous, guaranteed-full-ride (or nearly full-ride) colleges doesn't have to be intimidating. Remember, these seventy-five or so schools across the country *need* people like you to apply. You are a rarity, although you might not feel like one.

Most of these generous full-need-met schools have low acceptance rates, ranging from 4 percent to 50 percent of applicants. However, unlike with the famous scholarships, you're not competing with all students nationally. You're only competing with those considering this specific school, and even then, you're still not competing with all applicants.

The more selective the university, the more likely that you're only competing with students in your region, state, city, school system, etc. Many universities aim to have geographic diversity, as well as diversity in terms of public versus private high schools, rural versus city dwellers, etc. But this can only be achieved if universities heavily consider your city, state, and background. Yale consistently has students from all fifty US states—this can't happen without their prioritizing geographic diversity and assessing student applications based on where the students are from.

A Yale alumnus I know, Joe, seems to have benefitted from this. Joe's academic records were not the best since he only began to take his studies seriously in his junior year of high school. He attributes his acceptance into Yale to his background as a student from a small rural town with a small population. Being among the few students from his state applying to Yale, his main competitors were really only other students in his small state, and likely only those at private high schools like himself. Friends with experience at elite admissions offices confirm that this is likely true. He did also have unique experiences, having had few options for extracurriculars around him, given his low income in a rural state and small town. Joe wrestled competitively, played bassoon, and did nature activities with his local 4H club, a résumé of very diverse interests.

What does this mean for you? Just like college tuition prices, colleges' "acceptance rates" don't apply to everyone equally. You *can* get into these tougher schools. By being from the bottom half of families by income, you're already very unusual (i.e., unicorn). Studies show that students of equal merit and SAT scores but from lower-income backgrounds do not apply to these top schools. You are going against the grain.

Advantages you have:

1. **You aren't being compared directly with very privileged students.** Universities do consider life circumstances. When I applied, I had never been abroad, I hadn't learned any languages, I didn't have any prestigious awards on my résumé. I didn't even play the bassoon. But I did have a short but strong track record of helping disadvantaged communities and taking advantage of opportunities around me. I had volunteered to do taxes for low-income families, had an internship from my state's low-income youth matching program, and was a leader in my student government at community college, among other things. You're not being directly compared to high-income students whose track record might look more like spending a summer in Latin America building houses, interning at a family or nearby elite law firm, and winning awards in a skill or sport that depends on years of costly private lessons.

2. **You're likely diverse in some way that you might not realize.** Being from a rural area, a border community, underrepresented cities or states (i.e., not the Bay Area or Manhattan), single-parent household, child of immigrants or an immigrant yourself, from public school, etc. You might also be an unusual combination of interests or identities (say, a Mormon or Cuban American active in the Democratic Party, etc.) or have a story of triumph and personal change (former criminal record, high school dropout) that you can use to write a very compelling essay.

3. **Because you didn't start preparing for college since middle school or kindergarten, you'll show an intentional growth trajectory in your résumé.** Admissions officers love these, especially if your essay clearly articulates the reasons for your shift.

Even if you're already a high school senior or college freshman, you can optimize your academics and extracurriculars for the next two to four semesters until you apply to transfer into one of the schools offering huge automatic scholarships. If you're a high school junior, even better! Optimize your junior and senior years and apply to college your senior year. If you don't get in, use the "be an all-star" student route at a community college or public university, then apply again to transfer schools during your sophomore or junior year of college. You just have to make sure that the universities you desire do extend their financial aid guarantees to transfers.

LAUNCHING THE START-UP OF YOU

Thinking about getting into a top university can be scary. It might feel like a big leap, charting a path no one around you has done it before.

But here's the thing: you're in charge of your own life. You get to decide how to deal with whatever comes your way. Being passive is easy, whether you're rich or poor. But when you don't have much, taking control is more important. Yes, it might be scary and risky, but the journey and the results are worth it.

Imagine a start-up journey: a few years of relentless dedication, long nights filled with anxiety about the future, and then one day, a breakthrough. The start-up is finally thriving. It's somewhat self-sufficient, well-funded, and the founder can now focus on maintaining and enjoying their newfound success.

Like you, founders wrestle with learning new skills, prioritizing their time, committing to bold strategies, and nurturing an unshakeable belief that they will succeed against all odds. You're on the cusp of becoming an outlier, much like they are.

Perhaps you feel held back because you feel "average," especially if no one has ever told you that you are bright, smart, or have potential. But here's another secret: success isn't about how high your IQ is. It's about bouncing back, sticking with it, and treating challenges as a chance to learn. Students who think this way—who see their abilities as something they can change—do better than students who think intelligence is set in stone.

For example, praising kids for being "smart" has been discouraged recently because it's thought that it diminishes the child's effort and can also cause a fear of failure, since failure means that they're no longer "smart." Thus, a child might be more likely to develop a fixed mindset, in which someone believes their skills and abilities (like intelligence or talent in academics) are predetermined and cannot be improved.

Research shows that students with a fixed mindset get lower grades while those with a growth mindset, who see their abilities as fluid and flexible, achieve higher grades. Those with a growth mindset take a poor grade as an opportunity to be curious about why they failed, re-focus, and improve. A student with a fixed mindset studies *less* when faced with a poor grade since they've already labeled the subject as something they are not good at.[3]

So, what mindset do you carry?

You are capable of immense growth and change, but you must believe it first. Trust me, you are not predestined for a life you don't absolutely love. You have the potential to create something extraordinary out of nothing. The first step is to sell that idea to yourself.

This book isn't just about the steps to get into elite universities. It's about instilling belief in your abilities, especially when you've grown up with fewer resources. People in your shoes often grapple with self-doubt because they've rarely been encouraged to dream big. This book is here to change that.

The journey will demand sacrifices. Just like a start-up founder, you'll need to prioritize your goals over immediate gratification, trusting that the payoff will be worth it. You'll have to hustle, make bold decisions, overcome obstacles, and relentlessly move forward. But your hard work will pay dividends.

Consider Taylor Swift, who completely shifted her life to chase her dream of music. It required time, sacrifice, and an intense focus. She even postponed adopting her first cat, Meredith, until after her third album. But look at her now: leading her industry, owning her craft, and living her dream with three of the most loved cats in the world!

More privileged students often don't doubt their ability to gain admission into selective colleges because they've been told that it's expected of them. But who's there to tell you the same? I am.

Together, we're going to take those big goals and break them down into steps that you can handle. We're going to make the most of the time that usually devolves into doom-scrolling on

3   https://blog.prepscholar.com/how-to-get-a-4-0-gpa-and-get-better-grades-by-a-harvard-alum.

your phone or watching back-to-back Netflix episodes. Don't become another "could have been." Have the courage to bet on yourself and strive for an exceptional life.

By picking up this book and reading this far, you've shown determination and promise. You are capable of implementing the advice in this book, just like a start-up founder is capable of turning an idea into reality. You're armed with unique strengths and resilience—your seeming "disadvantages" are your secret weapons, sharpening your resilience and making you stronger. Now is the time to rewrite your story, to dream big, believe in yourself, and take that first step toward the future you deserve. It's not about where you begin, it's about where you're going.

DECIDING YOUR MAJOR AND OTHER BIG THINGS YOU DON'T HAVE TO WORRY ABOUT RIGHT NOW

Don't let the following keep you from applying to these financial-aid-guaranteed schools.

Not Knowing What to Major In: On college campuses, "What's your major?" is often the question that follows "What's your name?" You will hear it a lot. But you don't have to decide your college major until your junior year of college, typically. I went from being an art major to a liberal arts (i.e., pretty much generic or "undeclared") major during my first two years of college and switched to international affairs when I applied to generous universities for my junior year. The major I declared was different for each university I applied to because each school offered different majors. Also, I learned so much from my two years of extracurriculars and classes in different fields (public relations, marketing, economics, philosophy) that I had a much better understanding of which careers I wanted to pursue. You'll likely go through something similar, too. You might even be more competitive if you're flexible on your major; some schools have easier admissions requirements for certain majors!

How Bad You Did in High School: If you're reading this as a high school junior, senior, or super senior, you might feel there's nothing you can do to make up for a low grade point average (GPA), lack of extracurriculars, or perhaps even a criminal record. Your slate pretty much gets wiped clean once you start at any college, so consider taking some semesters at community college, as I did. University admissions officers will mostly only look at your college semesters, not your high school résumé. Your high school transcripts are submitted with your application more as a formality to ensure you graduated. (Note: If you've already started college and your grades are weak, you can always get them back on track. One of the students featured in this book, Alexa, went to community college for three years before going to an elite university. As mentioned above, your transcripts matter inasmuch as they demonstrate growth. Admissions officers like seeing improvement over the years and persistence in overcoming adversity, because these skills don't just set you up for success in school, they set you up for success in life.)

Your IQ: NASA Moon Lander Lead Engineer Ben Cichy tweeted about getting a 2.4 GPA his first semester in college. He'd begun to doubt that he was cut out for engineering—yet he still landed two spacecraft on Mars and is currently designing one for the moon. Don't think that because you had some bad grades in the past, you can't get good grades next semester or that you're not smart. A GPA is almost entirely based on time and effort. Think about what your school habits would look like if you received $10,000 for every A. You'd probably be class valedictorian. As I discuss later, each A is worth that much to you, if not more, and anyone can get them if they put in enough time. Hard work trumps natural talent/IQ/intelligence. The times I got low grades were because I hadn't studied and underestimated the class difficulty, or I didn't get essays reviewed early by my professors, so I didn't have a clear grasp of their expectations. Unlike so many defining factors of your life, grades are *in your control*. We'll go over how to minimize surprise bad grades and set up systems to get good grades in Chapter 4.

Not Being Superhuman, Perfect, or Highly Organized: I set my alarm for the wrong time and missed my scheduled debate in an important tournament that *my debate team flew me to*. I missed class multiple times due to car breakdowns because I made a bad choice about what car to get. I didn't use my time as efficiently as other top students because I didn't realize that working retail and restaurant jobs (rather than more "professional" but similarly paid jobs like on-campus or research roles) didn't count for much in college applications. Nonetheless, I still got into multiple full-need-met universities, including Yale, on scholarship. You don't have to be perfect to be the type of person who gets into top schools.

Not Knowing What Career You Want Post-Graduation: Even the renowned founder of Amazon, Jeff Bezos, wasn't sure what career to pursue and changed his major after exploring his fit for different subjects. If you can graduate debt-free thanks to hundreds of thousands of dollars in scholarships, you'll have a *lot* of career options to choose from. Plus, people change careers often. Your major or your first jobs don't have to be your forever career. Career choices most often look like this: you work in one sector for three to five years until you switch to something else that seems more impactful, fulfilling, higher-paying, or interesting. You'll learn about new niches, opportunities, and problems to work on throughout your career. I have friends who started off their careers by working in banking before switching over to research and policy work. If you want as much career clarity as possible, use your university years to test out different topics, types of work (i.e., independent research, journalism, data analysis), and employers (i.e., internships) on someone else's dime. Even if you decide to be (or do) something that doesn't require a bachelor's degree, like an entrepreneur, police officer, or writer, a bachelor's degree will help you stand out in that career and any career pivots thereafter. Life is full of career pivots. I personally think of my career in five-year chunks, regularly asking myself: What are the most exciting things I want to work on for the next five years? Find out how to get there.

Whether College Is Worth Your Time: You might think that you can learn what you'd learn in college on your own. I agree with you. You can read a syllabus for a fraction of the cost of enrolling in class. However, college isn't all about books or in-class learning. College is about getting experience, building relationships with people in different fields, and testing out careers as quickly as possible, at low to no risk to yourself or your livelihood. Internships, professional extracurriculars, and professor-supported research projects are usually only available to students. These programs were specifically designed to help students gain real-world experience and a better understanding of their chosen field, free of charge. Your college professors can become your biggest allies and supporters through this process. After college, there's no support system helping you test out employers and career paths. College also signals to employers that you're driven, disciplined, and have a broad base of knowledge.

Examples of opportunities you can only get as a student:

1. Think you might be good at working on pandemic prevention research? Ask your professor if you can do free work for their lab if there aren't any paid positions available.

2. Want to test if you'd enjoy journalism? Join the university newspaper and see if you'd do well as a writer, photographer, or editor.

3. Have you been curious about TV and media? Your school probably has an alumni network that can help introduce you to a local TV channel open to hosting an intern.

Throughout my summers, I tested careers by getting internships. Although my internship at a local TV station seemed exciting, the high-stress environment of the 5 p.m. news hour dissuaded me from the field. By gaining firsthand experience, I was able to recognize that it wasn't a good fit for me, sparing myself years of dissatisfaction. My subsequent internship at an immigration advocacy nonprofit was fulfilling, but it also illuminated the harsh realities of burnout within the sector.

Ultimately, my short tests of various careers proved to be a winning strategy. It set me apart from my peers and helped me get scholarships and prestigious diplomas that I can use to get future jobs, no matter what career I pivot to. Well worth my time.

CHAPTER 2

RANK SCHOOLS BY HOW MUCH MONEY THEY'LL GUARANTEE YOU

MAKE THE COMPETITIVE U.S. UNIVERSITY SYSTEM WORK FOR YOU

As of 2022, approximately seventy-five universities across America offer to meet full financial need (see the full list in Appendix A, pg. 162). You can also check for more updated lists by searching online for "full-need-met" universities. Of the 4,000-odd colleges and universities across the country, these are the only ones that you need to consider.

TARGET THE UNIVERSITIES THAT WILL PAY TOP DOLLAR FOR YOU

The first step to getting these *guaranteed* scholarships is to make a list of schools whose guarantees apply to you. Some schools meet all of a student's "**demonstrated financial need**" if the student's family income is below $100,000, while some schools might offer these promises only to families making $30,000 a year or less.

You can get a rough estimate of your family income by looking up the average yearly earnings for their job title. For example, cashiers earn on average $30,000 a year, while janitors, construction workers, and bookkeepers earn on average $40,000 a year. If you know your parent's hourly rate, multiply it by 40 (for 40 hours a week if full time) and then again by 50 (if they work for most of the 52 weeks in a year).

To get an accurate number, however, ask your parents about their income or ask for their tax return forms, though I know it might not be easy. For a lot of families, money is a really awkward and difficult subject. One way to make this money discussion easier might be to include your parents in your strategizing process and to fill out the financial forms and university financial aid calculators together.

In general, the yearly income on your parents' most recent tax forms is the income that universities will use to decide whether you're eligible for their promise of meeting full need.

If you're over twenty-four, married, have dependents, or are a self-supporting youth at risk of homelessness, you will likely be considered financially independent and can use your own tax returns.

If you're twenty-four years old or younger, but financially independent, you may need to work with that school's financial aid counselors in order to receive an exception. But it is possible! I have two friends who did this and got large financial aid packages.

Take some time over the next several days or weekends to research university financial aid promises to make your list of "dream schools."

1. Start with the schools on LendingTree's "**No Loans Colleges**" list and the list of seventy-five universities that offer full financial aid (see the full list in Appendix A, pg. 162). Google the schools on this list that sound most exciting to you. Perhaps you like the location, have a family member nearby, or love the dorms or Greek life. Spend time looking at these schools first.

   a. I recommend considering all seventy-five schools, not just no-loans colleges. As you'll see in the close-up of financial aid estimates toward the end of this chapter, some no-loans schools might calculate your financial need less generously than a school that considers loans, making the school that considers loans potentially cheaper.

2. To get more info on their promise, try googling: "University X full need met," "University X financial aid promise," or "University X financial aid guarantee." Fill out the university's financial aid calculator to get a sense of how much demonstrated need they calculate from your income data.

3. Make a spreadsheet. In each column, list the university, its cost (tuition + room and board), a rough estimate of the final cost to you after financial aid, and the acceptance rate. If this school meets all of your desires (you qualify for its

promise, you like the location, it has your general subject of interest), then also add early application and normal application deadlines.

    a.   If you're intending to do two to four semesters at another, cheaper college, also confirm transfer application deadlines and whether the promise also extends to transfers (this may require a phone call to the school's financial aid office).

	A	B	C	D	E	F
1	University	Cost	Cost after Financial Aid	Acceptance Rate	Extra Details	Need-Blind?
2	University of Richmond	$78,810	$6000 subsidized loan	28.80%	$5k for summer	Yes
3						

4.   Continue looking until you have fifteen to twenty schools from which to choose. *The typical US student applies to six universities on average.* Because you're aiming for only the most selective schools, apply to at least **twelve**. If you don't have a 4.0 GPA, aim to have as many schools as possible that have a 15 percent to 40 percent acceptance rate, rather than those that have an acceptance rate of less than 10 percent. If you'll be applying as a transfer student, confirm that the financial aid promises apply by checking out the financial aid promise details, filling out the university's detailed financial aid calculator, or calling the financial aid office.

    a.   I applied to sixteen schools and had no in-state backup. A tip from Harvard alum Lynette who applied to seventeen "full need met" schools and two in-state backups: *"I reused my essays for most of them and I got all the application fees waived, so it was a pretty cheap way to increase the odds of getting into at least one."*

5.   Check whether the universities near you have similar promises. Sometimes, the promises at local universities allow higher incomes because the promises are limited to students from that public school system or that city. For example, the University of Rochester's Promise Scholarship Program guarantees a full tuition scholarship to students from the local public school system, as long as their family

income is less than twice the area average ($137,400, or twice the $68,700 area average). The University of Rochester has a 40 percent acceptance rate. University of Texas at El Paso promises local students with family incomes less than $75,000 full tuition despite their 100 percent acceptance rate.

    a. Note that these *local guarantees usually don't include room and board* in the scholarship because these promises are for local students.

6. Keep track of whether you qualify for *application fee waivers*. Many schools use the Common App, where you can apply for multiple application fee waivers at once. For schools that use their own portal, you may have to apply directly with the school for the waiver. If the website is unclear or the application fee would cause hardship for circumstances not covered in the waiver guidelines, consider emailing the university directly requesting a waiver. Add a column called "Application Fee Waiver" with your notes.

    a. While you may get many application fee waivers, you might still have to pay out of pocket for test scores and financial aid forms. Start putting money aside (if possible) from your part-time employment as soon as possible. The total cost might be a couple hundred dollars—though this will allow you to compare *hundreds of thousands of dollars* in scholarships offers.

7. Cross-check your list with a list of **need-blind schools**. Start an additional column named "Need Blind" and add "yes/no." Schools that are not need blind will be harder to get into than their general acceptance rate because these schools can hold your financial need against you when considering whether to admit you. Need-blind schools keep the financial aid paperwork separate from admission. (Example list: https://blog.prepscholar.com/need-blind-colleges-list).

    a.   If you're planning to transfer, confirm whether their need-blind process applies to transfer students as well.

    b.   Based on the rejections I received from schools that were not need blind, I estimate that a school that does not have a need-blind admissions policy will make the acceptance rate about 5 percent more difficult. So, a school that normally has a 15 percent acceptance rate might be about as hard as a school with a 10 percent acceptance rate.

8.   Pick out four universities you're most sure you'll apply to. When you register for the SAT and/or ACT tests, you can send your scores to four schools for free. Sending scores to any schools after that will incur a fee ($12 for SAT, $18 for ACT in 2023). Add a column named "SAT/ACT" and mark these four as "to send during test." Since you can't see your score before it gets sent out, consider sending these four scores to schools with easier acceptance rates. (If you're unhappy with your score, you can retake the test and send just the better score.)

These are your lists of schools to aim for. As long as you get admitted to one of these, you'll get automatic large scholarships, and you won't have ridiculous student loans.

As you do your research to choose your favorite universities, keep a lookout for additional guarantees that some schools provide. The University of Richmond, for example, has a Richmond Guarantee program that gives every eligible student $5,000 for an unpaid or underpaid summer internship or faculty-mentored research project. Smith College has an Ada Comstock Scholar program in which they encourage transfer students to apply who are over twenty-four years old, a veteran, or have a dependent (other than a spouse), with support and flexibility to attend full- or part-time while living on or off campus.

IMMEDIATE FREE (OR CHEAP) COLLEGES IF YOU'RE ALREADY A SENIOR OR SECOND-SEMESTER JUNIOR

If you're already a high school senior or a second-semester junior with average or below-average academics, your best bet is to go to a local community college near you. If you are just now starting to devote yourself to being a competitive applicant, you won't have enough semesters to show growth and a track record of excellent extracurriculars and grades before you apply for colleges in the middle of your senior year.

I recommend community colleges over public universities to start because *community colleges tend to be very cheap* (around $3,000 per year) and tend to have a lot of power vacuums, making leadership positions easier to get with limited time (further details about optimal extracurricular strategies in Chapter 5). Universities might also be more excited about you because these selective schools get limited applications from community college students, making you more unusual. Lastly, community colleges tend to have counselors or offices devoted to helping students transfer to four-year universities, since community colleges do not offer four-year degrees.

Another choice would be a local public university. Leadership positions may be harder to get because most students expect to be there all four years—so best leadership positions likely go to those who have been around longer. Also, be careful of inertia: you could easily continue at this university until you graduate, never taking the scary dive into applying for far-away selective schools. At a two-year college like a community college, there's a clear need to take the plunge and transfer to a dream school.

If you're undecided between the university or community college near you, consider opting for the option that uses a simplified grading system without plus or minus grades. This means that only letter grades like A, B, and C are used in the final course grade. Maintaining a 4.0 GPA is much easier under this "flat" grading system. For example, if the community college considers grades such as A-, B-, and C-, it may require more effort to achieve an A because you'll need to consistently score above 94 in every class instead of just exceeding a 90 grade. This can leave you with less time for extracurricular activities and part-time jobs.

You can also decide based on whether the national Pell Grant will cover the entirety of your community college or public university tuition. The Pell Grant is free money (up to $7,395 in 2023–2024) awarded from the federal government to any U.S. student in good standing and has a qualifying income. To apply for it, just fill out the Free Application for Federal Student Aid (FAFSA). The FAFSA will also give you a more exact estimate of what schools might calculate as the amount your family cannot afford to pay, also known as your "demonstrated need." Fill out the FAFSA even if you think your family income is too high. Many factors are considered, like family size and being an early bird. Applying in the first three months when FAFSA opens, tends to lead to twice as many grants. Go into this with the assumption that they want to give you the funds.

Additionally, about half of US states offer additional community college tuition grants to qualifying students, making community colleges tuition-free. Check whether you qualify in your state by searching online for community college state grants or promises. See what you qualify for in other states as well.

Some community college students can even get guaranteed admissions to certain universities. In California, community college students who fulfill course requirements and maintain a certain GPA are guaranteed admission to several University of California schools. All University of California schools offer the Blue and Gold Opportunity Plan, meaning that California residents with family income under $80,000 will not have to pay tuition or fees out of their own pocket. Search online for California universities' "transfer admission guarantee (TAG)."

Also, check whether you are near one of the community colleges that are part of the Transfer Scholars Network, a program entirely dedicated to helping community college students transfer to one of the fourteen top four-year colleges that offer some of the nation's most generous financial aid programs.

As of 2023, Transfer Scholars Network community colleges include:

Florida:

- Broward College
- Indian River State College
- Miami Dade College

Massachusetts: Holyoke Community College

Mississippi: Mississippi Gulf Coast Community College

New York:

- Borough of Manhattan Community College
- LaGuardia Community College
- Queensborough Community College

Texas: San Jacinto College

Virginia:

- Northern Virginia Community College
- Richard Bland College

CLOSE-UP VIEW OF FINANCIAL AID GUARANTEES

Many of these selective universities provide online "actual cost of tuition" calculators, giving you a sneak peek into the potential financial aid packages they might offer. To help you understand the differences in their offerings, I tested a few of these calculators using a scenario: a fictional two-parent household earning $44,000 with one child.

The key takeaways? First, while some institutions may promise no loans, they could still expect a larger upfront contribution from you. Second, schools often factor in personal expenses and book costs when calculating financial aid, which means your actual gap—what you owe directly to the school before the semester begins—might be lower. You can typically cover these additional expenses with a part-time job.

If delving deep into the numbers isn't your cup of tea, feel free to skip this section. Just keep these main points in mind as you move forward.

If you're still unsure about college, here's a cool perk to consider: room and board (i.e., food) costs are a considerable part of the overall cost. But you'll have those expenses once you move out of the house, regardless of whether you go to university or not. So why not try to get someone else to cover as much of those costs as possible!

Colgate University (acceptance rate: 17.2 percent) promises to meet all demonstrated financial need of accepted U.S. students without using loans.

Colgate's Estimated Cost of Attendance

Tuition & Fees	$66,270
Room & Board	$16,588
Books & Supplies	$1,528
Transportation	$600
Personal Expenses	$1,084
Total	**$86,070**

You don't actually owe the school $86,070, though. You only owe $82,858, the combined total of tuition & fees and room &

board. Books, supplies, personal expenses, and transportation are costs you take on throughout the year.

Colgate's financial aid calculator suggests my fictional family of three would receive:

Estimated Grant/Gift Aid

Estimated Federal Pell Grant	*$5,845*
Colgate Grant	*$75,425*
Total	*$81,270*

The estimated grant aid is just $1,588 short of what you owe to the school: $82,858! The perceived gap between cost and aid appears larger because Colgate includes estimated out-of-pocket expenses for books and personal needs. However, you can spend much less than Colgate estimates, for example, by buying used books and selling them quickly (more cost-saving strategies on page 75).

Calculated Family Contribution	
Parent Contribution	*$0*
Student Contribution	*$2,000*
Potential Self-Help Opportunities	
Student Work	*$2,800*
Estimated REMAINING COST	$0

Colgate's financial aid calculator says these fictional parents are expected to pay nothing. However, most schools expect that even the lowest-income students work on campus or have a job before starting school to come up with roughly $2,000 remaining. You really have to come up with only $1,588 before the semester starts, though, since the rest of the estimated net price are your personal expenses over the course of the entire year.

Connecticut College (acceptance rate: 41 percent) also promises to meet all demonstrated financial need and offers a no-loans promise below a certain unpublished income thresh-old. The fictional family of three with an income of $44,000 didn't meet that threshold, though Connecticut College still ends up being very competitive. After financial aid, $74,241 in grants will help you cover the $79,900 you would have paid to the school, which amounts to an automatic scholarship of 93 percent.

Dive into this section if you're curious about how Connecticut College's calculator breaks things down, factoring in personal and book expenses for scholarship calculations. **Not your thing? Just head to the next page.**

Estimates for the 2022–2023 Academic Year

Connecticut College Tuition, Fees, Room & Board	$79,900
Books & Supplies	+ $1,000
Other Expenses	+ $1,600
Total Cost	$82,500

When I accessed the calculator in mid-2023, Connecticut College expected the fictional family of three with an income of $44,000 to contribute $3,809 upfront (Expected Family Contribution or EFC). Thus the school wants to help you cover all costs above your EFC ($78,961).

Your estimated grants and scholarships:

Federal Grants	
Pell Grant	*– $5,245*
Federal Supplemental Educational Opportunity Grant	*– $1,000*
Connecticut College Grants and Scholarships	
Connecticut College Grant	*– $67,996*
Your Estimated Net Price	*$8,259*

The school offers $67,996 (not the full $78,961) because federal grants help cover your need. The net price listed is not the amount you owe the school, as it includes the costs for books *and personal expenses, which total $2,600. You only owe $5,659 ($8,259-$2,600).*

I know this looks like a lot of numbers, but the numbers that matter most are as follows: You get *automatic grants and scholarships totaling $74,241*, which nearly covers the $79,900 amount actually owed to the school. For $5,659, you get room, board, and tuition for a full year. That's a fraction of the typical cost for one person who is not in college to eat and live for a year!

To pay that $5,659, though, the school also offered a $1,700 work study opportunity and a direct subsidized loan ($2,750) to cover almost half of that. Direct subsidized loans do not charge you interest while you're in school, and they qualify for some loan forgiveness programs and repayment plans. These are the most manageable loans available.

Occidental College (acceptance rate: 38.2 percent) also promises to meet full financial need. Even though they offer loans in their package, this same fictional family of three with a yearly income of $44,000 would pay roughly the same amount as at Connecticut College. Occidental College seems to calculate this same family as having less money to give as part of the expected family contribution (EFC), which makes up for their offer of a loan. The school is automatically offering $71,836, so my fictional family would have to come up with $6,060 to pay to the school directly. If they take the $5,700 subsidized loan offer, they pay just $360 up front.

Estimated Cost of Attendance

Tuition & Fees	$60,566
Room & Board	$17,330
Books & Supplies	$1,240
Personal Expenses	$1,500
Total	$80,636

Estimated Grant/Gift Aid

Estimated Federal Pell Grant	*$5,245*
Occidental College Need-Based Grant	*$66,591*
Total	*$71,836*
Estimated NET PRICE	*$8,800*
Calculated Family Contribution	
Parent Contribution	*$0*
Student Contribution	*$0*
Potential Self-Help Opportunities	
Student Loans	*$5,700*
Student Work	*$3,100*
Total	*$8,800*
Estimated REMAINING COST	$0

PAYING FOR THE LAST MILE OF COLLEGE COSTS

Minimize or avoid student loans for the so-called last mile of college costs:

- Apply for small scholarships (less than $2,000). If you have the résumé to get admitted into a selective school like Occidental College, you'll likely be able to get a few $1,500 local scholarships in the six months between being admitted and starting school.

  - More details on how to apply for small, last-mile scholarships are in Chapter 7.

- Spend two to four semesters at a community college to delay transferring into the university. You can transfer to most colleges up until your junior year of college.

  - If you qualify for the full Pell Grant, which is $7,395 in 2023–2024, community colleges that cost less than your Pell Grant award will end up free. The rest of the Pell Grant would go directly to you. Save this money for when you do transfer!

- Continue working your part-time job(s) to fill that $3,500 to $5,500 gap.
- Consider calling the university, pointing out that the expected family contribution will cause hardship. Explain any other extenuating circumstance that might not have been covered in the financial aid assessments.
  - Consider colleges that don't include loans as part of their "full need met" promise, though those might be harder to get into and may calculate your expected family contribution less generously.

Keep in mind that ~$6,000 for a year of university is still cheaper than the price of most public college tuition alone. This price accounts for room and board, which includes food. These schools often have generous funding for summer internships and travel, which might offset some or much of this cost.

If you end up with enough scholarships to cover all the required fees paid to the university (tuition, room and board), the subsidized loan might be sent to you in cash. Since the financial aid calculations use generous estimates for textbooks, transportation, incidentals, etc., this loan money gave me more than I needed. I put the loan money in a separate bank account and then paid the loan off in full the month I graduated. I didn't even need to touch the cash, since I kept working part-time jobs on campus.

Because government-subsidized loans do not accrue interest when you are in school, these can be interest-free loans as long you pay them back quickly. Decline that portion of the subsidized loan that would go to you in cash if you doubt that you'll be able to set it aside for true emergencies.

CHAPTER 3

YOU CAN BE A STAR STUDENT

DEVELOPING A BETTER
VERSION OF YOURSELF

As I navigated the college application process without a strong support network, I often felt like I was stumbling through the dark, unsure if my efforts would ever pay off. Family members and close friends questioned my priorities, insisting that I was wasting my youth chasing academic and extracurricular achievements. You might hear the same comments from people whose experiences have given them no other way to process what you're telling them. They might even remind you that some successful people, like Steve Jobs, dropped out of college. But I knew the more common scenario is the countless people who go through life struggling because they did not have a college education. I wasn't going to let that be me.

I knew that success wasn't going to just fall into my lap; I had to be like a start-up founder, making big decisions with incomplete information, going against the grain, and pushing forward every day. You have to **maintain momentum** on your projects, extracurriculars, and classes, despite what others around you say.

The beauty of it all is that being an all-star student doesn't mean fitting into a particular mold; it's about finding what you truly care about, building your own goals, and working tirelessly to achieve them. So don't be afraid to be yourself and forge your own path. You don't necessarily have to join sports if you don't enjoy them; you could work more on landing dream writing gigs rather than campus extracurriculars. Being a competitive "all-star" student that gets into top colleges is not about filling in any cookie-cutter template of what a student should be like; it's about exploring what you want out of life and building your personal life goals.

Some not-cookie-cutter student profiles of recent Ivy League school alumni (acceptance rates of less than 7 percent) and most selective school admissions (<15 percent):

- Taylor found out about Princeton's financial aid guarantee for his income level during a college fair in high school. He then focused sophomore to senior year on academics:

five to seven extracurriculars, president of two clubs, and great grades. Thanks to a high school teacher guiding him, he participated in a research program at a local university, where he got to do university-level research in high school. He spent summers working two jobs, nothing academic.

- Lynette was homeschooled and did a dual accreditation program in high school to graduate from high school with a two-year college degree. Along with maintaining a 4.0, she volunteered often and was part of the National Honor Society. She got to national-competition level with her history papers in National History Day (which she found out about via her teacher) and a simulated virtual business she ran for a Future Business Leaders of America national contest. Apart from one pre-law summer camp at Stanford funded by its financial aid, she worked regular jobs in the summers. She also participated in the college application preparation program Questbridge, which helped with her successful Harvard application.

- Justus got kicked out of a religious private school (for being gay) in the middle of his sophomore year of high school. He made an oath to leave his small hometown and realized that the universities that offered automatic financial aid are the toughest schools to get into. He focused on academics in his junior and senior years. He was a leader in drama club, a trivia competition team, and a student volunteer group for the local kids' Special Olympics. Despite not having many extracurriculars, he was deeply involved in three very different extracurriculars. He spent summers working low-wage jobs and had great grades. He wrote about getting kicked out of school in his admissions essays and is now a Yale alum.

- Alexa went to the only college she could afford out of high school, UC Santa Cruz, even though it didn't have the major she wanted. She learned that it was possible to take community college classes and then transfer to another university. She took community college classes for three years, maintaining a 4.0, while working multiple jobs and internships and founding a club on campus. She got into University of California Berkeley (14 percent acceptance rate), which offers all California residents with family incomes under $80,000 free tuition and fees.

■ Stafford taught himself to code and got friends who code to start offering coding services together in high school. In college, he helped professors do research on the parts of chemistry he was most excited about. Despite a lack of focus on grades (B average), he still got into a Yale PhD program.

If you're curious what the background of a lower middle income student who gets into multiple Ivy Leagues (including Yale and Princeton) right out of high school looks like (*note: you do not need to aim to do this*):

■ Casey got A's in all IB (International Baccalaureate, similar to Advanced Placement (AP)) classes, ran five after-school groups, did varsity for two sports, volunteered with CAP (a pre-military and teen leadership program), and did karate. He also started community college evening classes in middle school (programming). As far as he knows, he was the first person from his hometown to apply to an Ivy League.

> To become a top-performing student, you don't have to take on responsibilities that don't excite you. *Instead, seek out and create opportunities that spark your passion and align with your personal goals.*

However, you'll have to take ownership of your time and make short-term sacrifices. You may delay luxuries like moving out of your parents' home, getting a nice car, or owning a pet; remember that these are things that you can have, and that you might enjoy yet more, later. Keeping your expenses low means you also minimize the hours you spend working. Fewer hours at work means more time for your academic pursuits and extracurricular activities, some of which may be boring, but others of which will make you happy. Remember, invest in yourself now to reap the benefits in the long run.

WHY MOST STUDENTS DON'T AIM TO BECOME OUTLIERS

Throughout college, students periodically reached out to me for advice on how I came to be so involved on campus while juggling part-time jobs. Few of those students seemed to be able to change their habits. Similarly, I once gave a lecture to a group of university students in which I spoke about how I came to win a national fellowship. When I showed a screenshot of my calendar week, people were shocked and dismayed by my packed schedule, although all I had really done was block off when and where I would study, eat, and do tasks for my extracurriculars. Instead of feeling inspired to test out a different time management approach and get out of their comfort zone, they clung to more familiar ways of going about their days, usually with little to no time management at all.

After reading a lot of psychology books and findings, especially about willpower, I conclude that these are the main reasons that those students didn't take more steps toward becoming actively involved in school:

1. **Life is fine the way it is.** Some students didn't desperately need scholarships—so any hustle didn't really make sense from a cost-to-benefit ratio angle. Someone (perhaps a parent or trust fund) paid for their university, so they weren't going to rack up tons of student loans. There wasn't any compelling reason for them to aim for top schools that give massive scholarships.

2. **No burning desire to leave home and experience a top university.** Apart from getting scholarships, I really wanted the experience of going to an out-of-state top university: living in a different part of the country, studying abroad, experiencing dorm life and fancy dining halls, and befriending other students who were also driven. Despite not being a college-track student in high school, I had big

dreams. I wanted to be around others with big dreams, and I figured that other people with big dreams were at top universities.

3. **No burning desire to prove yourself.** When I transferred from my public university to a community college, people asked me if I was dumb, found university too difficult, or if I was pregnant. I was in fact trying to work fewer hours so that I could implement my college scholarship strategy. I wanted to prove that not only was I smart enough, but that I could go to schools more exciting than my local university.

Keep these fears in mind as you go through the (at times) lonely journey of building up the start-up of you. You are rare, but you are not strange for going all in on making this dream a reality. In other words, a unicorn. Watch out, however, for the mental obstacles listed below that can keep you from learning just how far you can go.

1. **Fear that if you try, you'll fail:** This is probably the biggest and most common fear. For example, I have a friend who dreams of becoming a writer, but he has never begun writing his book nor creating a plan to publish it. He claims that the profit-driven publishing industry would never accept a book like his, and so he tells himself that it's pointless to even try. By clinging to this narrative, he avoids the risk of failure and can continue to hold onto the belief that he's a talented writer held back by an unfair world. He's also ignoring the option of self-publishing. Once you try and fail, you can no longer comfortably blame the system. This can make trying, with its risk of failure, seem terrifying.

2. **Not Having Seen Other People Succeed:** It's hard to see that your dream life is possible if you haven't known other people to achieve it (whether that is a certain career, a twenty-five- to thirty-hour workweek, or owning a business). If you haven't met and befriended people who have tried out for the Olympics, written a book, or received

massive scholarships, it's easy to wrongfully write off these dreams as things "other people" do, those who are "unlike you" in some significant and unfixable way.

3. **Fear of investing time without a clear and immediate pay-off:** If you doubt that working hard in school will lead to a big payoff, you're less likely to see a reason to try hard in school.

These fears are almost entirely based on your circumstances and the norms in which you grew up. If you had grown up like my friend Harvey, who was surrounded solely by people with great degrees and professional careers, you would not question whether you, too, could get into selective universities. I especially dealt with fear #3 daily, up until the moment I got my scholarship offers. These fears come with being that rare lower-income student breaking glass ceilings, the downside of being the underdog.

To make your dreams seem achievable, aim to get internships that will allow you to meet people in your dream profession as soon as possible. To help with your confidence, focus on schools that guarantee full financial aid and have easier acceptance rates, like 30 percent to 50 percent. You can definitely get into one of these by focusing on your academics and extracurriculars! Also, even if for some reason you don't, the extra work you did to aim for these will help you stand out when applying for jobs, other universities, and private scholarships.

If it helps, remember that you're not obligated to tell your classmates, coworkers, or friends about your grand plan. Few people knew which schools I'd applied to. The first time my friends heard the words "Yale" and "I" in the same sentence was the day I got in.

HOW SHORT-TERM GRATIFICATION CAN DERAIL BRILLIANT STUDENTS—AND WHY YOU WON'T BE ONE OF THEM

Some of my friends tried to copy my strategy, and they came fairly close, but there was something invisible that held them back.

My friend Aria got nearly perfect grades throughout community college while surviving solely via her minimum-wage job—an impressive feat. However, during her first years of college, she decided to take out a loan for a *very* expensive new car and a dog. With these additional monthly expenses, she didn't have time to do any extracurricular projects. She had to take on a lot more hours each month to keep up with the car payments. Getting the dog, Arkyn, during college made her unable to move into dorms, since no one in her family could take Arkyn. Because she wanted some portions of her dream life as soon as possible, she tied herself back.

Being future-oriented can make or break this college strategy. These big financial commitments derailed her ability to be flexible with her time and location.

And unfortunately, being present-oriented seems to disproportionately affect lower-income students. This is not because these students are fundamentally different from anyone else, but because they lacked opportunity to build this skill.[4] Studies show that lower-income students are more likely to be raised in situations in which delayed gratification didn't make as much sense—you're more likely to eat whatever food is in the pantry today, rather than save it for later, if you know from experience that there may *not* be food in the pantry tomorrow. You're more likely to splurge on expensive purchases in the few instances you have $200 (or $2,000 for that matter) in your bank account, if having large lump sums of money is a rare occurrence.

---

4   https://www.washingtonpost.com/news/wonk/wp/2016/06/08/the-problem-with-one-of-the-most-popular-assumptions-about-the-poor/.

This present versus future orientation even seems to impact parenting habits: Indiana University sociologist Brea Perry found that low-income parents are more likely than affluent parents to give in to their kids' requests for sweet treats. Other studies have shown that "poorer parents try to indulge their kids when they can, while more affluent parents tend to make their kids wait for bigger rewards."[5] This doesn't mean that you have to be born into money to learn how to save it. The takeaway is that just like creativity or muscle mass, patience is something that anyone can develop with practice—it isn't a talent that was factory-installed into a rare few.

To my friend, buying an expensive car and getting Arkyn was part of getting her dream life, and she wanted that life immediately. She would have waited if she had been sure that investing her time and energy in college would lead to a higher income later and a better life for herself and her dog.

Future orientation doesn't only impact big financial commitments like getting a new car and pet. It impacts whether you spend your free evenings, and your precious income, on things that feel good now—like social media and entertainment—instead of things that will make your future easier, like searching for better jobs, putting in extra effort to turn your B grade into an A, or signing up for the debate team. Although it might be hard to imagine, you have a very long future ahead of you, many decades that could be full of travel, financial freedom, and fancy dog walkers if you want, all because of your actions now.

CREATING URGENCY AROUND SCHOOL

Creating sense of urgency is essential for reaching your goals, staying motivated, and jumping toward intimidating opportunities. You can intentionally ignite your inner drive and create your own sense of urgency around academics. I built my sense of urgency by keeping in mind two things:

5   https://www.theatlantic.com/family/archive/2018/06/marshmal-low-test/561779/.

- *If I get straight As for the first four semesters of college, this would pretty much guarantee me over $200,000 in scholarships.* This means that each and every one of those twenty As (four semesters; five classes per semester) was worth $10,000.

- Wealthy families are willing to pay $200,000+ for a degree at a top university to give their child a world-class network and experience, as well as signal that they're a top student. *I'd be getting the same experience as those paying $200,000+ for less than the cost of my local university* if I play my cards right in these two years *before* applying to top universities.

This is the same type of urgency that valedictorians and star students tend to have, either due to parental pressure or intrinsic motivation. Due to this urgency, I saw school as a platform to achieve my deepest goals and even a game that I could play in order to stand out and get on my dream career path.

REWRITE YOUR STORY: EMBRACING YOUR JOURNEY AS AN UNDERDOG

Don't feel guilty about not having been a great student in the past. It's a waste of time, as it does you no good. The star students you saw around you likely had trusted adults in their life to remind them, sometimes constantly, of the payoff for school performance. If you are reading this book, you likely didn't have that.

A lot of things went into my friend Harvey having the confidence and know-how to apply to top universities without a second thought. Similarly, you might have been pigeonholed into a specific track by your school system or the people around you.

1. **Gifted and Talented, Pre-AP, and AP programs disproportionately recruit from higher-income families; not being in these programs doesn't mean you're not**

smart: A lot of smart kids don't end up in these programs, solely because the gifted/talented track in America is based on IQ tests that are most often requested by well-off parents. When a Florida county piloted a universal screening of students, 80 percent more black students and 130 percent more Hispanic students entered gifted programs.[6]

2. **Your high school counselor may have made assumptions about your academic capabilities and future goals, leading them not to flag selective colleges as a potential step for you:** My high school counselor assumed I wasn't college material. Since I was ahead in my required course load, she recommended that I graduate a year early, though with a degree that would have made me ineligible for college. She might have gotten this impression because, despite doing well in pre-AP classes, I declined AP classes because of the $100 test fees. If someone had explained to me the benefits of taking them, I would have explored ways to pay the fees. Your high school counselor may have just assumed you were not college-track.

3. **No one, including you, sees you as capable of being a top student:** I am someone who constantly misplaces my phone and has more than once left the remote control in the refrigerator. I did not think I was the type of person to get into Yale, and I almost didn't apply. I had to learn that getting into these universities is nothing more than a function of how much time you put toward academics and building *confidence*. Lower-income students with similar test scores, grades, and extracurriculars tend not to apply to schools as selective as those considered by similar but higher-income students. Fortunately, confidence, like patience, is something that anyone can develop: you'll gain more confidence as you see yourself succeed in class and extracurriculars. You'll soon see yourself as someone capable of being accepted to a selective university; even if you don't, you should apply anyway, as I did, since your application fees are waived!

---

6   https://www.washingtonpost.com/news/wonk/wp/2015/09/22/these-kids-were-geniuses-they-were-just-too-poor-for-anyone-to-discover-them/.

OVERCOME LACK OF CONFIDENCE

My friend Chaker achieved remarkable success in his early twenties by writing and publishing a best-selling fiction book, then traveling the world to speak about its themes. When I asked how he knew he could achieve this at such a young age, he said a book-writing goal didn't seem so unusual since both his parents were published professors. This example shows how our parents' norms can guide us more than our education or extracurriculars. In my friend's case, his parents' invisible script made writing a book seem like a natural next step, even though it's a daunting feat.

It took me a long time to gather the courage and confidence to commit to writing a book. However, meeting Chaker, who was not much different from me, played a significant role in breaking down my limiting beliefs.

Be on the lookout for people you admire in your circles who can tell you more about their journey. Is there a small business owner you admire in your community, a fellow student who seems to get more done in a day than you do, or a relative who has things in her life that you want? People love to talk about themselves if you show a genuine interest in them, and the priceless motivation they can offer you is free of charge. Ask questions, find a connection between you and them, and surround yourself with people who strive, and your momentum will build.

To take this advice to the next level, try spending more time with individuals who are actively striving to improve themselves or their lives. By spending more time with people who are willing to take risks and bet on themselves, you'll feel less alone or unusual in your own journey. However, this doesn't mean cutting off friends who may be facing challenges.

In addition to finding inspiration from people who have achieved similar goals, another powerful tool is to imagine yourself in a "you're perfect" suit. Here's a question posed by one of my favorite authors, Ramit Sethi. He said, ask yourself: "What would I do if I thought I was perfect?" This mental exercise helps you see yourself as not too different from your hero, giving you the confidence to explore how they achieved their dream. Once I gained the confidence to pursue writing a book, I delved into researching the process, finding online resources, and studying the outlines of my favorite books. As I broke down the process into manageable steps, I realized how achievable writing a book could be.

Put on the "I'm perfect" suit daily, especially when you consider getting involved in things that seem scary at first, like going to your first club meeting, running for student senate, or introducing yourself to faculty, staff, or other people whom you admire. Remember, all they have to go on is what you tell them; what you tell them is what you're telling yourself; and what you need to tell yourself is: *I got this.*

CHAPTER 4
GET TOP GRADES

ACE CLASSES WHILE STILL HAVING A
SOCIAL LIFE

Now that you know that you are capable of becoming a top student, set up the **habits** and **systems** that will get you there. Daily habits and systems, like checklists, time-blocking, and routines, are key to getting top grades efficiently. Daily routines might sound boring or might seem as though they will get in the way of spontaneity. However, these systems actually allow you to *enjoy* your life by making sure you spend time on the things that matter. In my six years of university, with all my extracurriculars and focus on grades, I only *once* pulled an all-nighter—and I made and kept friends that I will have for a lifetime.

Overall, if you are at a school that uses flat grading—i.e., no plus/minus (like A-, B-, C-) and only A, B, C—shoot for a 4.0 GPA. A 3.7 is more realistic if your school uses A-, B- C- (an A- is typically scored as a 3.7).

Top grades are possible if they become your top priority. This means that you'll have to do unusual things, like keeping track of your grades throughout the semester, often by checking in with professors.

Most of the strategies in this chapter work well for both high school and college students. At the end of the chapter, I include some strategies specific to college students.

REFRAME GRADES AND LEARNING

As I mentioned earlier, I envisioned each A as being worth $10,000.

Really take a moment to visualize this. Think of the dreams that $10,000 would make a reality. How would you approach classes if you got $10,000 in cash for every A? You'd do your homework first thing once you got home, set up a daily study habit, and proactively check in with your professors about your projects and grades to ensure there were *no* surprises.

You'd also choose your classes differently. School is a great place to learn, but for $10,000 you could buy a lot of textbooks, pay for a semester in Europe, and have car repair money that would ensure you got to school on time. You probably wouldn't take a chance on professors who are known for being difficult graders, ones who only give an A to three students in the class, regardless of how many students worked hard.

If you pretend to have that sense of urgency, everything else will fall into place. And in some ways, you really *are* getting $10,000 for every A. Having straight A's at the end of your two or four semesters can become $200,000 in automatic scholarships by getting you into selective schools with financial aid guarantees.

With this mentality, the strategies in the rest of this chapter will feel easier to implement.

OPTIMIZE YOUR CLASS SCHEDULE FOR GPA AND ENERGY

Avoid having more than one excessively demanding class during a semester, especially if you're in college.

If possible, *avoid needlessly difficult professors.* You'll get little extra kudos for taking the same course with a professor who requires very time-intensive work, rote memorization, and hardly hands out A's. That detail and your extra effort won't show up on a transcript. Ask upperclassmen or, if you're in college, use RateMyProfessor.com to get a better sense of the teacher's or professor's teaching style and time-intensiveness. Even if the course was on a subject I really liked, I wouldn't imperil my GPA with an instructor who took pride in making classes excessively demanding (typically, other instructors teach similar courses and may offer a more manageable workload). Some teachers might quiz you on unimportant details from the textbook chapters because they've decided they value knowing you have read the textbook unnecessarily closely, rather than engaging with the core material efficiently. If you are required to take a course with an excessively demanding or time-intensive instructor, make sure that that is the only excessively demanding course you do that semester.

Sometimes classes are excessively time-consuming because of the course's topic. Organic Chemistry and sometimes even an entry-level class like Intro to Physics or Calculus can be very difficult, no matter the professor. *Make sure to prioritize to do well on these foundational courses.* Count this as your one excessively heavy class per semester. (Note: Avoid saving challenging courses for the final semesters of high school or college, since colleges prefer to see a grade improvement over time. A bad grade might hurt you less in the beginning of your school record rather than toward the end.)

Relatedly, keep track of the deadlines to drop a class without getting a mark on your transcript. Add the deadline to your calendar. If you find that a class is unexpectedly taking a lot of time, find a better way to make up the credits and drop the class.

For high schoolers:

Take AP and IB courses, since selective colleges generally expect that you challenge yourself with what's available to you. Do not, however, aim to take every single AP class available. Selective colleges don't expect students to overload themselves with AP classes.

As PrepScholar.com, a website that specializes in university admissions, notes, schools expect you to take AP courses in the courses that are your "specialty."[7] If you focused on science and math, consider taking AP science and math courses but don't cause undue stress to yourself by taking AP economics or literature, if you're not excited about the subject. The same concept would apply for a humanities-focused

---

7   https://blog.prepscholar.com/how-to-get-a-4-0-gpa-and-get-better-grades-by-a-harvard-alum.

student considering doing AP science courses. The time spent struggling through the AP science course can be better spent on an energizing extracurricular, a side project, sleep, or a more enjoyable AP class or two.

Plan ahead by mapping out which courses you'll take for the rest of your high school time, especially since some require prerequisite classes.

HOW TO ADDRESS DIFFICULT ASSIGNMENTS OR LOW GRADES

I was surprised to find out how many students spent excessive hours doing calculus homework when our community college had free calculus tutors on a walk-in basis. Looking online and asking other students are *not* the only ways to get unstuck during difficult assignments.

- Check what your school's tutoring program offers. Most students aren't aware of the free tutoring resources.
- Ask the instructor or instructor's assistant for help.
- *College students:* Go to the professor's office hours.

Also, online artificial intelligence language-based models like ChatGPT[8] can help give in-depth explanations of difficult concepts. For writing, you can use these to generate essay ideas and get over writer's block. Use this carefully, however. Sometimes these AI models are wrong; do not use them to cheat, as professors are starting to use AI model detection technologies too.

Pro tip: You can use these AIs to bump up your extracurriculars, too! I use OpenAI's GPT/ChatGPT for writing letters to politicians on issues I care about, coming up with chapter titles, and changing the tone of emails or any other text.

8   Available at https://openai.com/blog/chatgpt/.

If you understand the class concepts well but you find that you're struggling with assignments, consider exploring what your instructor wants students to get out of the class. A big part of getting great grades is also optimizing your work to what the instructor expects—and the instructor's high-level expectations aren't always clear from the syllabus. For example, some instructors might want you to focus on rote memorization of dates rather than decade-by-decade trends.

I had one design professor who wanted students to create a very exact example of a common design principle and valued proof of long hours of work (similar to how architecture students endure long hours to build meticulous 3-D plans), rather than a focus on the theoretical understanding. This professor valued application much more than theory, though some professors will prefer theory.

Some instructors might want your essays to be in line with mainstream thought, while others might be disappointed if you're too mainstream. Once, I asked for the professor's feedback on my essay draft only to realize from the professor's reaction that my essay needed to align with his more mainstream opinion rather than the direction I had taken. If I hadn't submitted the essay early enough to rewrite it, I would have received a low grade for not meeting the instructor's unspoken expectations.

If you know you studied enough and had a good grasp of the material but still didn't do well on an exam, ask for your instructor's advice on improving your study focus and strategy. Come prepared with a well-thought-out list of the areas you want to improve on. By taking this approach, you'll show that you're eager and ready to acknowledge your shortcomings, act on feedback, and work extra hard. Do not ask for special treatment, like an additional chance to take the test or extra credit only for yourself.

KEEP TABS ON YOUR GRADES

Ensure there are no surprises when it comes to your grade: check in with the professor periodically for an estimate of what your final grade will be. Another thing to throw into the calendar and forget about until you have to do it. You have a right to know, and they have an obligation to take the time to tell you (they will appreciate your active engagement in your own education and will tell you whether it's good news or bad news). Making a habit of this keeps you in the driver's seat and will bolster and encourage the study practices you're developing.

Switch into high gear mode if you're not on track for an A. Get help from the professor to understand what concepts you're struggling with, review old exams, and improve your note-taking strategy (incorporate flashcards, take more detailed notes, and perform a better review of them, etc.). Understand what the instructor expects and prefers so that you can improve how you do on assignments. Author Tim Ferriss would famously spend three hours in person seeking clarification from his professors or their assistants whenever he did not receive an A on a writing assignment.

Strategically choose to spend more time on classes that aren't in "safe A" territory. Similarly, consciously shift to not aiming for an A+ if an A+ doesn't boost your GPA any more than an A.

Review the syllabus closely to keep track of any extra credit and assess which kind of work contributes the most to the final grade. Spend more of your time on the work that impacts the final grade more, with the awareness that this may not be the more enjoyable work. Our brains are hardwired to avoid less enjoyable work, so intentionally focusing on these tasks is essential.

OPTIMAL SCHOOL WORK SYSTEM

Consistently getting A's comes down to two main things: doing schoolwork every single day, and doing schoolwork in ways that maximize your retention of the critical information.

Making time to do schoolwork each day. I didn't think of any day as a day "off" from schoolwork. Yes, this includes Sundays, national holidays, and my birthday, while school is in session. By schoolwork, I mean homework, assigned readings, reviewing lecture notes, etc. Doing *at least* an hour a day of schoolwork, every single day, was my default mode during semesters. It was no longer a decision about "should I study today"; rather it was "what time do I begin doing my first task of the day: schoolwork." Even on weekends, starting on schoolwork was my default first task after eating breakfast. This has the added advantage of freeing up the rest of your day for fun.

By setting up a daily habit of doing schoolwork, you're pretty much guaranteed to not have to cram your homework, readings, and studying right before class or the exam. Not only will you do better in the class, but you'll also retain what you learned longer, and the extra sleep is life-changing.

Setting up the habit of daily focus is crucial. Academics depends on your structuring your own time, particularly in college since you might have an entire weekday without a regularly scheduled class.

While most days should consist of working on your goals, use your same daily and weekly structures to make time for fun and downtime. Everything is stronger when your life is organized—including your friendships and social life. A good rule of thumb is to make plans to eat a meal with friends most weekdays. Set a regular time (every Tuesday at 12 p.m.) to put it on autopilot.

Step by Step: A Daily Time-Blocking and Checklist System. It can be tricky to ensure enough time for all your classes. As a rule of thumb, each reading or homework-intensive class will require two to four hours a week each week. To keep yourself on track, I recommend using a daily system that combines the following:

1. **Checklists:** Either write a daily to-do list in a notebook or use a to-do list app (like ToDoist, Any.do, or Reminders). In the apps, you can even set up recurring to-dos to read for each class.

   a. Pro: Checking off your school tasks as completed is satisfying.

   b. Con: It doesn't ensure you'll have the time to do the tasks for that day (hence, pair it with time-blocking).

2. **Time blocking:** Every evening or every morning, plan out what you will do during your blocks of free time, including giving yourself breaks and time for lunch, exercise, and having fun. I usually did this by putting it in my Google Calendar or writing it in my school notebook, in the very back pages, where I could refer to it easily. In the notebook, I also included any non-school-related tasks to remember to do throughout the day.

   a. Pro: Time blocking can give you a more accurate sense of how much you can do that day and ensures your hours align with your priorities.

   b. Con: You will likely stray from this daily plan, and you may stray often. Just reorganize your day and continue.

Doing schoolwork in ways that maximize retaining the critical information: Like most things in life, this isn't not about working hard, it's about working smart.

1. Take memorable notes while you're doing the assigned readings. Think about what you read as you're reading it; see if you can paraphrase the material for someone who hasn't read it. Ask questions or respond to the material (e.g., "Napoleon conquered most of Europe but was finally

defeated by...the Russian winter? Didn't see that coming!" "The Cuban Missile Crisis almost started WWIII but was resolved in just 13 days? Cutting it close there!"). These notes are 90 percent of the reason you're doing the assigned readings. Bring these notes with you to class to help you contribute to class discussions. These notes are also critical study material for quizzes and exams .

    a.   Taking notes on PDF articles is much easier if you use a PDF-highlighting app that allows you to export just the segments you highlighted.

2. Use the Anki flashcard app for classes that require memorization (such as language classes, anatomy, and organic chemistry especially). Anki is probably still useful for history and liberal arts classes, though you don't want to get too hung up on choosing what concepts to put on flashcards. However, creating flashcards is time-consuming. Make creating flashcards part of your review, use AI or ChatGPT to put your notes into an Excel-type format you can import into your flashcard app, or potentially ask people on Fiverr or Upwork to make the cards for a fee.

3. Work on math homework daily. Math problems are nearly impossible to cram. Working on them early will allow you to know which questions will require office hours, tutoring, or asking a friend.

4. For science classes, usually your goal should be to understand the lecture material and *apply* it rather than focusing on doing all the assigned reading. Increase background reading only if you struggle to follow along in class. Find the balance between being prepared and being efficient.

5. Use a note-organizing app like Evernote, OneNote, or Notion. Use the "tag" or "journals" features to separate each class to ensure you don't miss a note when you're studying for that class.

OPTIMAL STUDYING

1. Study in fifty-minute increments. Have a study plan for every study session. Build a study plan that breaks each study session into smaller, specific chunks. Take ten minutes out of your fifty to write down how you plan to study and create a checklist to track progress.

2. Explain topics to yourself in different words, as if you're explaining them to a friend. I still pretend to explain policy issues to my friend Aria to prepare to give policy briefings. Engaging the material in this way helps your brain recall and absorb the material.

3. Review the notes you made from all the assigned readings. Make important segments bolder so they're easier to review.

4. Review Anki flashcards throughout the semester, not just the week before exams. Anki has a nice feature that auto sets a minimum daily flashcard review, so that you'll have a spaced-out review of all the material. Make that part of your daily checklist.

5. Study by yourself. Studying with friends might be more fun, but you likely won't study as effectively.

6. Make sure your study includes information from every class or lecture. If you miss class because of car or bus trouble, sickness, or a family emergency—which, as I explain below, are the only reasons you should miss class—reach out to the instructor for the slides, ask fellow students for the notes, and ensure you understand that day's lecture.

7. Get as much information as possible about what will be on the tests. You can either infer this by analyzing what's been on prior tests or even by asking the instructor or former students for prior years' tests (if the instructor is okay with this).

8. Focus some of your study on your prior errors and wrong answers on tests, assignments, or essays. Make sure you

know why you got each answer wrong. This is especially critical for STEM coursework, in which concepts in earlier classes are foundational for doing well in more advanced coursework.

9. College students: Always go to study sessions offered by your teachers or their assistants. Even if you feel great about the material, study sessions are useful because they tend to focus on what's going to be on the test. Sometimes, tests won't focus on what you expect, so by going to the study session you'll get a heads-up. Also, attending these sessions (which professors and teaching assistants are under no obligation to organize) shows that you are engaged.

MULTIPLE-CHOICE TEST STRATEGIES

Hours before a very important Texas-wide standardized exam that determined which students moved forward, my third-grade teacher shared some tips with our class that I've used on multiple-choice tests ever since.

- Since tests aren't made to be completely random, choose C if you're in a four-options test and have no idea at all what the correct answer is. This will also prevent you from wasting precious test time on impossible questions.

- Answer the easy questions first. If you think a question will take two or three minutes more to answer than the average question, mark that to come back to it later. With this strategy, if you run out of time, you'll have used your time efficiently, since all questions, even the easiest ones, count for the same amount.

- Similarly, keep a mental note of how long you can spend on each question. If you have sixty minutes for a thirty-question test, aim for a two-minute maximum on each question. Leave questions needing more than two minutes until the end.

- Before turning your test in, check your answers. Sometimes, during my review, I found that I had accidentally circled a wrong answer or even noticed a trick question. At the very least, check that you filled in every bubble.

Hack Your Willpower

I was shocked when I found out some students didn't go to class simply because they didn't feel like it. Especially if you're in private school or college, tuition is very expensive, and every hour of class is probably $50 to $100 at least. I realized the students had broken their streak or shattered their identity as someone who just *always goes to class*. They had established a norm that questioned whether they *should* go to class. Because they no longer had the identity of someone who *always goes to class*, attending future classes became a decision requiring mental processing.

Do not ever miss class. Once you miss a class, it will take willpower to go to class, rather than just being a default, automatic thing you do. Remembering that semester when I could barely keep up with paying my tuition, I felt grateful for the opportunity to attend class—don't lose this hunger.

Life hack: Establish the habit of staying on campus between classes and until the end of the day. My college roommate Marjie would intentionally plan 1- to 2-hour gaps between classes so that she would be forced to stay at her community college campus. This helped her get into the mindset of doing schoolwork as well as making it easy to go to study sessions, tutoring sessions, and instructor's office hours.

By going to every single class, extra sessions, and office hours, you'll develop your identity as a good student, building momentum and strong habits. You'll also see that class becomes much easier when you engage actively with it in this way, rather than try to figure things out on your own. A great side benefit is also that professors will notice your diligence and likely be more open to recommending you for opportunities (like internships) and sending strong recommendation letters to universities. Professors are on the lookout for promising students to root for and support.

Hack Your Motivation

My dirty secret: I don't rely on motivation because motivation varies by the hour, day, and week. Don't expect to rely on motivation for more than a day or so.

Use those days that you are feeling motivated to set up a better accountability system for the days that you're not feeling motivated (a tip from Ramit Sethi). Accountability systems will force you to do what a motivated version of you wants "unmotivated you" to do.

Accountability tools I use (choose one to try out this week):

- **Focusmate:** With this online platform, you pre-commit to co-work virtually with another person for twenty-five or fifty minutes at a specific time. This helps to provide structure and support for your goals. If you don't show up, you get a lower "dependability" score, and you force your partner to get another, last-minute partner. You get three sessions a week for free, or unlimited sessions for $10 a month.

- **Freedom:** Probably the most important app on my laptop and phone. Freedom blocks social media and Reddit during my prime distractable hours (10 p.m. until the next day at noon). I no longer stay up late browsing social media, and I no longer delay getting out of bed by scrolling. One additional perk is that when I wake up at night, I end up opening a meditation app or reading an e-book instead of getting on social media.

    - Setting up Freedom is a big commitment. Start out with a smaller set of hours if blocking it for fourteen consecutive hours seems intimidating. I started out blocking for ten hours, then found that I really enjoyed my day when I was more present and doing things that aligned with my goals instead of scrolling. Typically, you will still be able to send non-photo and non-video messages on Messenger and Instagram, for whatever reason.

To try after the two above:

- **Routinery:** This phone app helps you build and maintain a routine. When I wake up or when I am doing my bedtime routine, I know exactly what my next steps are. I set my evening routine to (1) Tidy my space for sixty seconds. (2) Time block the next calendar day. (3) Write in my journal for two minutes. I recommend an evening routine that includes (a) checking for any outstanding homework or readings; (b) reviewing flash cards; and (c) planning the next day (either on paper or your virtual calendar). For Sundays, I recommend setting a longer, say a two-hour routine, during which you research universities, look for new volunteer opportunities, or apply for small scholarships to support you until you get into your dream university. End the Sunday routine with something fun, like watching a TV show, calling a friend, or other self-care.

- **Beeminder:** Beeminder is one of the most powerful, if not *the* most powerful, accountability tool available. You *will* achieve your goals because you're betting money on yourself. If you don't meet your goals, the app will charge you. This book would not exist without Beeminder: I established the habit of writing this book by having Beeminder charge me $5 if I didn't add five hundred words to the Google Doc with my draft each week. Beeminder had access to the Google Doc and could verify directly whether or not I had met my goal.

  - I've also used Beeminder to ensure that I do the following:

    - Do one or two items from my to-do list (via Beeminder's integration with the ToDoist app)

- - Spend less than two hours a day on social media (with the time-tracking app Rescuetime integration)
  - Run once a week (via Beeminder's integration with the Runkeeper app)
- You could start using this app to hold you accountable for other things:
  - Reviewing online flashcards (with the Anki app integration)
  - Signing up for three Focusmate sessions a week (via the Focusmate integration)
  - Reading one assigned reading for each class each day by typing in the name of the class that you read for (no outside app required)

- **Stickk.com:** Similar to Beeminder, this has native support for one-off commitments, and you can have the payout money go to a charity or an individual. You can easily add a third person who can verify that you succeeded.

- **Boss as a Service:** This one won't appeal to everyone, and it might be out of your budget. For $25 a month, you can get your very own "boss" to hold you accountable for the goals you want for that day, week, or month. The "bosses" tend to be quite encouraging, pinging you to make commitments if you haven't made them yet. It's similar to a life coaching service, but more affordable than an actual coach.

Signing up voluntarily to lose money or take on a personal boss might sound bizarre, but some people I know who most fulfill their goals use tools like this, especially if their work is self-directed, full of important but unpleasant tasks, or otherwise "start-up"-like. Keep in mind that you are building a start-up of you: be open to all the tools and resources out there for you, and invest in yourself wisely.

ESSAY WRITING

All writers have a healthy fear of the blank page. This is surmountable—all you need is a plan of attack that works. As follows:

1. Get feedback early from your professor. This means you have to come up with a thesis and a rough outline quickly. You should do this as soon as the essay is assigned, ideally on the day of the class in which the professor mentioned it. You brainstorm better when the course material is fresh in your head. Avoid falling into the trap of starting an essay on the night before it is due just because some other students may do so.

    ▪ Run your thesis by your professor before you even start writing it. Better yet, see if you can form your thesis with your professor. If possible, also run your essay outline by your professor.

2. Turn in essays early for feedback. I would finish essays two weeks early to request that my professors give me feedback. I've found this early review process to be the only way to get A's consistently on essays. Set this "early deadline" on your calendar and ensure your to-do list includes working on this essay.

    ▪ If your instructor doesn't allow turning in the essay early for feedback, ask if they'd be willing to review your essay outline.

3. Use AI-powered Elicit.org for literature reviews. I also found Google Books to be a great resource for building a literature review and getting book sources easily (rather than only using internet-based sources). Google Books (books.google.com) shows pages of many books and even allows you to search text within books. With Google Books, you can diversify your paper or research sources to also include books without having to go to a library or check out e-books.

The following are strategies specifically for college students:

BEST WAYS TO GET THROUGH EXCESSIVE READING ASSIGNMENTS

Some professors assign more reading than is humanly possible. This makes striking the balance between reading and skimming important. Especially since, unlike in high school, college students are sometimes tested about items that were only in the reading and never came up in lectures.

Ways to absorb the material quickly:

- Efficiently skim by reading the first and last page of every single chapter. Then, only reading the chapters that seemed most relevant to the course or class discussion.

- Search for comprehensive summaries of the book. Check Google, Scribd, and even ChatGPT for a chapter-by-chapter summary.

- Look at reviews and criticisms of the book, like Amazon or GoodReads reviews for more insight.

- Use text-to-speech apps (like Readwise Reader, Speechify, Pocket, etc.) to turn an ebook or PDF into an audiobook that you can listen to at 1.5x to 3x speed while doing other tasks, like walking or doing chores. These usually require a downloadable PDF or e-book version of the book, rather than Kindle.

  - A few ways to find downloadable versions of assigned readings:

    - Type a few words from the text, *exactly as they are written*, into Google, in quotation marks. If you're using the title, add filetype:pdf to get fewer results. Sometimes authors, publishers, or universities will post long reports, chapters, or even entire books on their websites for sharing.

    - Check Scribd. Scribd often has legal downloadable versions of books.

My favorite text-to-speech app, Readwise Reader, gives students a 50% discount.

Never Get Caught Not Having Read the Book Because It Didn't Seem Worth the Money

My most common approach: Get access to the syllabus in advance of the class (sometimes it's listed with the course listing, sometimes you have to ask the professor). Weeks before the class, email the professor asking if you can use an older edition. Order the older edition online.

Use BigWords.com to find cheaper textbooks. BigWords finds the cheapest way to buy the combination of books that you need by searching on many book websites. At the beginning of the semester, find and order online all the books you need for the semester by reviewing class syllabi.

You'll save money by ordering these online before you need them AND you won't lose time waiting to find the book when you're under pressure from a deadline.

If you can't afford them all at once, you can also wait to buy the book once it's clear that the book will be used in class. Sometimes professors assign books in the syllabus that they don't use in class.

Before buying through BigWords.com's search engine, I also like to do a quick check of these places to find e-books and physical books for free.

- Check the local library, both their e-book holdings and their physical holdings.
- Check Openlibrary.org and Scribd.com, the latter is by paid membership only but you could use a free trial.
- Use WorldCat.org to check nearby public and private libraries for e-book or physical holdings.
- If you only need a chapter or two, check if Google Books (books.google.com) has that book for viewing. If that

chapter is not available but other chapters are, grab any sentence from the book and search for it (using quotation marks) within Google to see if there are any electronic versions of the book archived anywhere.

- Check Gutenberg.org for over 70,000 free downloadable ebooks in the public domain.

- If you have a friend in class, you could potentially borrow their book a few weeks before they will start reading it since you'll have a daily reading system that will make it easy to read ahead of schedule, and remember: most students don't take as proactive an approach as you are going to do, so you have a superpower that they don't. Just make sure to take good notes.

Other options:

- Check Craigslist, Facebook Marketplace, and local listings. I used my college's university bookstore less than five times total during school.

Sell your textbooks at the end of the semester! Their worth will decline quickly when new editions come out. Don't hold on to them for keepsakes unless you're sure you'll reference the book again in the future. And even then—you won't. By doing this, I've even made a profit on a textbook by selling it on Craigslist for more than what I bought it for on Craigslist.

CHAPTER 5
BE THE PERSON WHOM UNIVERSITIES FIGHT OVER

STRATEGIC EXTRACURRICULARS TO
WIN ADMISSIONS BATTLES

Extracurriculars are as important, if not more important, than grades. Whereas grades get you in the door, extracurriculars make you unique.

Extracurriculars are also the key to helping *you* get the most out of school. Extracurriculars let you *build leadership experience, test out a career, make an impact, build marketable skills, develop expertise* (i.e., research), or *fuel your passion*—for free or cheaper than at any other time in your life.

Examples of the types of extracurriculars I did:

Leadership-based: Student government. Despite being nervous about holding elected office, I advocated for student interests and led a large social impact project supporting Ugandan schoolchildren.

Testing out a career: Summer internships at a local public radio station and a news channel station.

Impact-based: Volunteering directly with low-income communities via volunteer income tax preparation.

Skills-based: Debate team to improve my public speaking and critical analysis skills. Side perk: I got to travel to California and New York with the team!

Research-based: By focusing my research and writing assignments on poverty and sociopolitical issues in low-income countries, I not only garnered invitations to speak at school panels but also leveraged this expertise in my college and scholarship application essays.

Passion-based: Leader in art student society, helping organize a yearly gallery show.

Some extracurriculars will help you with several of these. For example, my art student society role (passion-focused) built my event-organizing skills. My college roommate excelled in literature competitions, which both fueled her passion and her writing skills. Also, you can be a leader in whatever group you join, as editor of the school paper, the head of Take Back the Night, or a decision-making role in the film club. Whatever will give you a nice title, take it.

Based on my informal interviews with numerous alumni, students with fewer extracurriculars are more competitive if their extracurriculars vary from each other and ideally cover all these types of experiences. Exploring a few very different sectors is good and unique, like our bassoon-playing wrestling Yale alum Joe. Also, don't fret if you aren't a star in sports, music, or any specific skill—most alumni I spoke to weren't, either. A lot of students apply with those extracurriculars, so they're not as unique or as helpful as other extracurriculars you can begin now.

SETTING UP YOUR STRATEGIC EXTRACURRICULARS PLAN

In the next pages, we'll walk through how to brainstorm specific opportunities to pursue that help you with your goals. Then, you can review which opportunities are available to you specifically. For example, by checking out school clubs and nonprofits around you, you'll build a map of what leadership opportunities you could take on campus. Even in towns of less than 10,000 people, you can find or create rich extracurriculars.

As a rough back-of-the-envelope estimate, aim for holding one leadership-based or demanding extracurricular (president of a large club, elected member of student senate, debate team) plus one or two substantive but less demanding extracurriculars (volunteering with an organization, being a research assistant, having a side project, etc.) at all times, plus productive summers (an internship or volunteering). Paired with a high A average, you should get into schools that have a 15 percent to 30 percent acceptance rate and are need blind. If those schools are not need blind, this should get you into universities with a 20 percent to 50 percent acceptance rate (since these schools will hold your financial need against you at admissions).

By consistently aiming to juggle three extracurriculars, getting hired for an internship, volunteering or doing a research project during your summers, and always being on the lookout for opportunities, you should end up with a list of eight or nine interesting extracurriculars by the time you apply for top universities.

Keep in mind, you can switch up your extracurriculars over the course of the year, especially since some have conflicting schedules. I didn't apply to be a student senator until after I did a semester of debate. Being on the debate team (which traveled multiple times a semester) was not doable while being a student senator.

While I know that minimum-wage work builds essential skills such as public speaking, managing difficult situations, and multitasking under pressure, do not count your minimum-wage work as one of your core three extracurriculars. It doesn't distinguish you well enough, as a lot of people in your income bracket will already be trying to use their jobs in this way. Nonetheless, feel free to mention your part-time job(s) in scholarship and college applications, especially if it took up a significant portion of your time. I had years of experience working in the restaurant industry as a server, and retail as a sales assistant across different sectors like electronics, shoes, and fashion, but I didn't make these the defining highlights of my college applications.

BRAINSTORM POTENTIAL ENERGIZING EXTRACURRICULARS

You might now have a broader sense of potential focus areas or what you want to get out of your extracurriculars. Let's come up with a plan for extracurriculars that is both energizing and exciting to you, get you closer to your professional or life goals, get you noticed by top universities wanting to give you scholarships, and ideally, make use of your existing skills, passions, or any other comparative advantages you have.

Get a piece of paper or a note-taking app and make a big list of at least fifteen extracurricular ideas. Put a star next to those where you have a comparative advantage, like considerable experience or foreign-language skills. Pull from the following types of examples:

Professions that you'd love to test out or get better at.

Medicine, writing, veterinary, TV, film editing, fashion design, robotics, video game development, ROTC

Research topics to work on, issues that have impacted your community, and causes for which you would advocate.

LGBTQ rights, a higher minimum wage, walkable/bikeable neighborhoods, affordable housing, pandemic prevention, road traffic death prevention, climate change mitigation, global poverty (roughly 10 percent of the world population lives in extreme poverty—meaning those who live on less than $1.90 a day—according to the World Bank), access to clean water, criminal justice reform, increased support for mental health and addiction services, improved services for sexual assault survivors, increased access to healthcare

Things you like, including (but not limited to) things you are good at.

Singing, sewing, sports, debate, chess, math, yoga, history, poetry, slam poetry, theater, photography, American Sign Language, French or other foreign language, politics, music

Favorite nonprofits.

Civil rights organizations, homeless shelters, a political party

Side projects.

Computer programming a small app, playing music at local hospitals, writing a children's book, starting a YouTube or Tik-Tok channel to explain pressing global issues

STRUGGLING TO BRAINSTORM? MAKE THE WORLD'S PRESSING PROBLEMS YOUR NICHE

Not sure what you're into yet? That's okay! Having a niche can really help you dive in and beat that tough first step: getting started. Try this hack: focus on problems that no one's solved or even noticed yet. To find those hidden gems, I like to check out 80,000 Hours, a nonprofit started by an Oxford professor. It's like having a secret treasure map to the world's most over-looked, neglected problems.

Some issues they highlight as pressing global problems are below. *This is a long list so only skim the bold titles.* Read the descriptions only if your interest is sparked.

1. **Risks from artificial intelligence**: The development of AI is likely to influence greatly the course we take as a society. If it goes badly, however, it might pose an existential threat.

2. **Catastrophic pandemics**: Biotechnological developments can make deadlier pandemics possible, due to accidental leaks or malicious use of man-made pathogens.

3. **Global priorities research**: Investigating how to prioritize global problems and how to best address them.

4. **Nuclear war**: Despite some progress, we have not reduced the threat of nuclear war enough.

5. **Institutional decision-making**: Can the decision-making processes of the most powerful institutions be improved?

6. **Climate change**: Beyond the suffering it's already causing, climate change will increase existential risks from other causes and affect standards of living far into the future.

7. **Great power conflict**: War between great powers (e.g., China and the United States) seems like one of the biggest risk factors for existential catastrophe.

8. **Risks of stable totalitarianism**: If a totalitarian regime ever becomes technologically advanced enough and gains enough global control, might it persist indefinitely?

9. **Space governance**: Even as investment in space increases, we have very little plan for how nations, companies, and individuals will interact fairly and peacefully there.

10. **Improving incentives and governance for global public goods**: There are many public goods problems in which no one is incentivized to do what would be best for everyone. Can we design mechanisms and institutions to mitigate this issue?

11. **Factory farming**: Every year, billions of animals suffer on factory farms, where standards of humane treatment generally range from low to nonexistent.

12. **Easily preventable or treatable illness**: Preventable diseases like malaria kill hundreds of thousands of people each year. We can improve global healthcare and reduce extreme poverty with more funding and more effective organizations.

13. **Mental health**: Depression, anxiety, and other conditions directly affect people's well-being. Finding effective and scalable ways to improve mental health worldwide could deliver large benefits.

14. **Spread of misleading and false information on social media**: The algorithms that social media companies employ to curate content may be contributing to harmful instability and erosion of trust in many societies.

15. **Voting reform**: First-past-the-post voting is common in high-stakes elections like those for the US president. Everyone who works on voting theory agrees that this is one of the worst systems there is.

Why are these problems considered so pressing? With few people focused on them, you can make an enormous difference by joining in. Even small improvements in these fields make a big difference, impacting millions given the global scale.

Another way you can develop an incredible niche is to focus on solutions with the most impact potential - even within your topic of study. In global health, some interventions like vaccines and anti-malaria mosquito net distribution are 50 times more effective than others. Eighty percent of lives saved seem to come from only 20 percent of interventions.

You can highlight those game-changing solutions. For climate change, convincing one person to take one fewer transatlantic flight achieves over ten times the impact of axing plastic bags. In broader climate policy debates, green tech research appears very neglected. Research into better green tech solutions receives very little funding - $22 billion annually versus $140 billion for clean energy solutions deployment subsidies. Experts say we should equalize research and deployment money. Advances in green tech could dramatically transform how we use energy and cut emissions.

According to 80,000 Hours' research, some of the most impactful and neglected areas within various fields include:

- Medicine: Medical research for diseases that affect the world's poorest people and pandemic prevention
- Climate: Green energy technology
- Computer Science: Artificial intelligence safety research
- Political Science: Nuclear weapons, voting reforms, and biosecurity

Don't be afraid to apply this same type of 80/20 reasoning (also called the Pareto Principle) within your existing field to find opportunities for efficiency and impact.

Choosing one or some of these issues doesn't mean you have to work on them forever! You can always pivot to something else, but just getting started on an interest, and keeping an open mind about it, can help you test out topics and careers more quickly.

You might end up working on multiple issues—and that's great! I ended up doing unpaid internships and volunteering in TV, radio, art, civil rights advocacy, teaching English, global poverty, and personal finance. I still ended up being able to focus on diplomacy, global inequality, and emerging technology, issues I fell in love with after working on them.

NOT READY TO DIVE INTO ANY TOPIC? DEVELOP SOUGHT-AFTER SKILLS

If you're undecided about career direction, consider skills like writing, problem-solving, or negotiation, which will make you in-demand for a wide range of impactful and/or lucrative careers like policy, consulting, and business. See the graph for in-demand skills:

Which skills make people most employable?

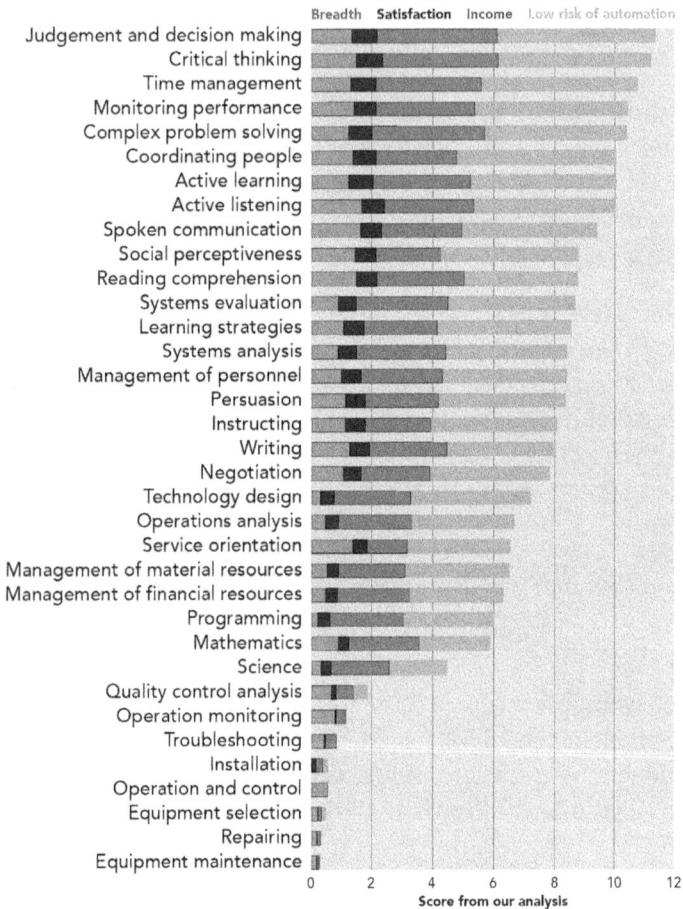

Breadth **Satisfaction** Income Low risk of automation

Skill	Score from our analysis
Judgement and decision making	
Critical thinking	
Time management	
Monitoring performance	
Complex problem solving	
Coordinating people	
Active learning	
Active listening	
Spoken communication	
Social perceptiveness	
Reading comprehension	
Systems evaluation	
Learning strategies	
Systems analysis	
Management of personnel	
Persuasion	
Instructing	
Writing	
Negotiation	
Technology design	
Operations analysis	
Service orientation	
Management of material resources	
Management of financial resources	
Programming	
Mathematics	
Science	
Quality control analysis	
Operation monitoring	
Troubleshooting	
Installation	
Operation and control	
Equipment selection	
Repairing	
Equipment maintenance	

Score from our analysis: 0 2 4 6 8 10 12

80000hours.org/articles/**skills-most-employable/**

A majority of these most sought-after skills are "soft" skills that involve working well with other people. These aren't typically what you learn in college classes—but it's what you can develop through your extracurriculars.

Examples:

- Student senate: coordinating people, active listening, judgment and decision-making

- Debate: persuasion, spoken communication, critical thinking

- Chess club: critical thinking, judgment and decision-making, complex problem solving

- Robotics team: technology design, complex problem solving, systems analysis

- Sports team: coordinating people, monitoring performance, time management

- Theater: spoken communication, active listening, social perceptiveness

- Model United Nations: negotiation, persuasion, critical thinking

- Programming club: programming, systems analysis, mathematics

- Math club: mathematics, critical thinking, judgment and decision-making

FIND OR CREATE STELLAR EXTRACURRICULAR OPPORTUNITIES AROUND YOU

Ideally, by now you'll have a list of at least ten potential topics of interests, including some specific niches of interest. Let's hone it down to a list of five real extracurriculars by exploring what is around you and reaching out to organizations.

The most important thing to remember is this: *get out of your comfort zone.* Joining student government, debate, and volunteering with strangers has always felt, to me, like something "other" students do—not me, as someone who leans introverted and was considering an art major. I chose these to get out of my shell and improve my public-speaking skills.

Formal School Clubs

Check out two to four school clubs. Ask your school for their list of clubs. Pick out a few that interest you. Go to each club's meetings to see what projects they do during the year, whether you enjoy the vibe, and whether they have leadership positions available.

Some smaller schools, like my community college, might not have clubs geared toward unusual passions (mine were singing, animation, global poverty). Thus, I focused on more skill-based extracurriculars (debate, student senate) and developed passion-based projects outside of school.

Consider starting or running a student club. It is not as complex or time-consuming as it may seem, especially if you already know how clubs work at your school. Your school likely offers resources to launch your own club. You'll be improving the campus culture and tailoring a club to your interest, as well as showing off your leadership capabilities.

Starting a local chapter of a national organization might be easier since you might get support from the national organization. Several national groups have local student chapters, such as Students for Sensible Drug Policy, Students Against Destructive Decisions (formerly Students Against Driving Drunk), and the Wildlife Society. Some groups, like the Center for Effective Altruism, provide discussion materials or book club resources.

Alternatively, you can initially take on a lower leadership role in a club, like treasurer or poetry editor, and gradually work your way up to running it if you find the work fulfilling.

Working with Existing Nonprofits

If a lot of your interests align with advocacy or volunteering, focus on getting involved with existing nonprofits.

Via Professors:

The best way to get interesting volunteer opportunities is to ask your instructors for ideas or introductions, particularly those teaching in your favorite subjects. I asked my international relations professor in Virginia whether he knew of any advocacy organizations at which I could volunteer or intern. Despite having no ties to Texas, the professor found an incredible immigrant advocacy center in my hometown in west Texas that could use my language skills for translations. I have many other friends with similar stories of finding the perfect opportunity via a professor.

Via Direct Contact to Local Nonprofits:

If you don't have an instructor to ask yet, or asking them didn't lead to any ideas, search online for local nonprofits working on your interests. You'll have better luck with local nonprofits, since national nonprofits tend to have more students reaching out to them.

Reach out to three to four local nonprofits asking if you can volunteer. If their website lists their volunteer training dates, sign up. Some smaller groups might not have regular training dates or a clear way to volunteer. If that's the case, offer to take on a specific responsibility for them like social media management or website management. You don't need extensive coding experience for this. User-friendly website builders like Wix, Squarespace, or Strikingly can help you build a website the group can manage even after your departure.

I joined two small organizations using these approaches: One, I had reached out to because their issue was a topic I had read extensively about so I could help with writing longer pieces. The other organization, I offered to take charge of their social media and online presence.

Via Direct Contact to Local Chapters of National Nonprofits:

You can get a prestigious big-name nonprofit on your résumé by going through a local chapter. For instance, the American Civil Liberties Union (ACLU) has a chapter in New Mexico, while the climate-focused Sierra Club has a Rio Grande chapter that serves both New Mexico and West Texas. At smaller chapters, you may be able to take on a leadership role early on (e.g., by volunteering to take ownership of a small project or lead a subcommittee). Subcommittees might be groups of fewer than five volunteers working on recruitment, membership engagement, or fundraising.

Typically, I find that being highly engaged and helpful to a local nonprofit or local chapter of a nonprofit can be done in less than three hours a week. Because so many of the volunteers have full-time employment and may be even raising children, these nonprofits tend to be very considerate of time. Meetings are often only once or twice a month, lasting about an hour each time. The other two to three hours a week are usually talking with potential partners or new members, drafting letters, or managing data, websites, or social media.

Via Direct Contact to Local Chapters of Political Groups:

Consider local partisan groups like your city Democrat, Republican, Libertarian, or Progressive parties. These tend to be highly organized machines doing interesting work. These can offer a wide variety of ways to volunteer, like writing, canvassing, public speaking, digital strategy, and operations. You can get a great mix of experience, plus a team that wants to help you improve your skills, so that you're more successful in helping them—which will in turn help your career.

Smaller political roles, like precinct chair for a political group, often go unfilled, presenting a prestigious opportunity with little competition. There are elected positions for most political groups for every precinct, which is roughly every block of 1,100 people. These positions focus on flagging local issues and coordinating with the larger political party. I know of a college freshman who is precinct chair while handling his full course load and extracurriculars at an Ivy League. The time commitment is fairly small (less than two or three hours a week) especially considering how helpful this is in building your network, reputation, and leadership experience.

City or Community Government Boards

Often, city and community government boards that oversee subtopics of interest to the city council or the mayor have unfilled slots. Sometimes these slots are even earmarked for young people or people within a very specific district. There's much less competition for these than you would expect. You'll get a very unique opportunity for your résumé and also likely see firsthand how difficult and complex achieving change in government can be.

National Nonprofits without Local Chapters:

Engaging with national and international nonprofits (without a local chapter) is more difficult. These tend to be nonprofits focused on issues at the national level, so they might not need as many people for local tasks, city engagement, or small-scale advocacy. The key is to be creative and to not be afraid of rejection. Here are some ways I've seen friends get opportunities at national or international nonprofits.

- Asking instructors or other contacts for any connections and introductions to groups in this field, highlighting that you're willing to work for free. I became a temporary research assistant for the World Bank (a renowned international non-governmental organization) by asking my professor if I could data clean for free for a World Bank project he mentioned during class.

- Save the nonprofit time by coming up with a helpful task or project that you'll do. Reach out to a volunteer coordinator or someone at the organization with the concrete idea. This might not lead to any opportunities at first, but you establish a relationship with the organization and could potentially get more involved later. Some suggestions:

- "I'm interested in fundraising at my school for your nonprofit. Are there any specific recommended methods for students to fundraise?"

- "Is there local advocacy I can push for in my city/state specifically?" (especially if you're already volunteering with a political advocacy group)

- "I'd like to write an op-ed about your recent work for my school or city newspaper. Would you find this thesis (insert main sentence/idea) to be helpful?" (especially if you already have an op-ed published somewhere to show)

- "I have a group of students interested in piloting a student chapter of your organization. Are student chapters something your group has been exploring or would be interested in? If not, we might start a student group focused on advancing your goals. What can we advocate for that would be most helpful to you?"

Make a good impression and commit to this, just like you would a more structured extracurricular (i.e., consistently do one to three hours of work a week; set up Focusmate to ensure you do the work on time if need be). You'll develop a relationship with the nonprofit and stand out, especially since nonprofits often have volunteers quit or flake out after two or three weeks.

Life hack: If you get a chance to serve on an admissions board or help with recruitment in a group you join, grab it! It's super helpful to see things from the other side. When you're writing your own university applications later, you'll be able to picture the people reading them. That can make a big difference!

CREATING YOUR OWN RESEARCH/NICHE OPPORTUNITIES

The same method of reaching out to strangers at established nonprofits can help you create your own extracurricular opportunities with private businesses, your favorite authors or online influencers, elected officials, anywhere really. If your interests lead you to zero in on some entity or person that isn't an established nonprofit, consider reaching out to them, making it clear how well you understand their work, field, or mission, and what you would like to do to be helpful to them. For example, I know of another Ivy League freshman who is an intern at one of the most influential and well-respected niche blogs in their field. They didn't achieve this by applying to an internship opening and competing with thousands, if not hundreds of thousands, of other students. The blogger didn't even have an internship program. The student got this internship by DM'ing the famous blogger and asking if they could write for them.

The key to creating your own opportunities and getting cool roles specifically created for you: cold emailing, confidently and competently.

This confidence is one of the things that top college consultants and Ivy League parents teach their children. An elite, Ivy-League-educated consultant told me that lack of confidence and unwillingness to toot your own horn to your idols is one of the key unwritten scripts that hold low-income students down, even when they're more capable than the high-income students.

This strategy requires a mindset shift, putting on your "What would I do if I thought I was perfect?" suit. When you momentarily pretend you're perfect, you think and act differently, more confidently. With this suit, emailing a faraway expert or offering to help a research team is less intimidating.

Putting on your "I'm perfect" suit could be the difference between coming off as confident and competent versus selling yourself short during calls and interviews. When you put on your "I'm perfect" suit, you're able to:

- Be less bashful about highlighting improvements that happened specifically because of you. *At my last job, I noticed and fixed these inefficiencies, saving us five hours a week.*

- See opportunities others don't see. *I bet I could help my favorite blogger with her blog. I'll reach out offering to improve their blog's first page or test out making video content.*

- Put yourself out there and make your own luck. *Of course an email to this famous blogger is worth my time. The worst that can happen is they'll ignore it or say no.*

- Keep trying and don't take it personally when things don't work out. *This blogger I love didn't respond. I'll email another five bloggers with specific offers on how I can help them, and I'll test out different ways to write that first email.*

- You improve your skills without doubting yourself. You don't take it personally when you need to learn better cold email techniques. Rather than assuming that everyone knows how to email busy strangers, you intentionally critique and improve your cold email skills. Any failure can be fixed by improving your strategies, rather than wondering if you're good enough.

  - Note: Emailing busy strangers with concise, thoughtful emails is a skill you can develop quickly. Wealthy students tend to have family members who can read over their draft emails to ensure they are written in a way that makes it easy for the busy person to reply. If you don't have family or friends with a lot of experience sending emails to busy strangers, research tactics and examples. I recommend you google *I Will Teach You to Be Rich*'s article on "How to Connect with Busy People."

Cold emailing confidently and competently works because a lot of jobs don't get advertised or even created until someone has an idea. Many thought leaders, authors, and research teams appreciate when someone takes the time to deeply understand their work and proposes ways to support their mission without taking up too much employee time or management resources. This approach can be particularly successful in securing positions like a research assistant, as university grants often allow for flexibility in the number of assistants. Similarly, social media or online content jobs may also be open to hiring part-time or freelance team members, especially if you can quickly prove that you'd add value as a part-time or freelance team member in their niche.

Typically, the trick is showing that you will be self-directed, internally motivated, and won't need hand-holding or lots of extra management. For most busy people, wasting time is more painful than wasting money. If you can clearly add value without subtracting time, you'll stand out a lot.

The following practices will help you persuade an organization to let you join their team:

- Researching what the target team needs. Do this by reviewing their publications, newsletters, and website, or doing in-person volunteering to get to know the organization. For example, after following an activist group for a while and volunteering at some of their events, I got an overall sense of how their email newsletter outreach and usability could be improved. For university research teams, this might look more like asking the team (professors, grad students, research assistants) about their work or any items on their to-do list that they'll never have time to get to, which you could offer to do for free.

- Develop a concise, easy-to-read pitch focused on the team's needs. The biggest mistake I see people make is sending a message trying to make *themselves* sound interesting, and explaining *why* you want to help them. Many interesting people want to join their team, so your wanting to join, as badly as you might want to, doesn't make you more valuable to the team. You're more valuable if you can make their life easier, either by proposing a helpful plan that you're capable of doing or by generally offering to do high-quality free work with little need for oversight.

STARTING UP A DREAM SIDE PROJECT

Starting up an independent side project in school is very difficult because you'll be very time-constrained, and you'll need to keep yourself accountable. I only recommend a solo side project if you've had a burning desire to do this project for years. The most common solo side projects are probably writing a book and starting some kind of start-up-like project or app. The hardest part is breaking down dreams that seem wild into very achievable subtasks. Skip this section entirely if you haven't had your mind on any solo projects.

Book Writing: Writing a book might sound scary. I broke it down by having a plan to write 1,250 words five days a week for twenty days. Writing 1,250 words takes about an hour, two hours if you take longer breaks and don't use a very detailed outline. By following this plan, I wrote the book in a month and took six months to have others review and suggest improvements. The most important part was the outline! I spent a whole week making the outline as detailed and clear as possible, which made writing 1,250 words much simpler, since I knew exactly what to write next. For a clear, step-by-step plan on how to write and self-publish a book, I recommend Matt Rudinsky's *You Are an Author*.

Writing and publishing a book like this one took about eight months.

Self-publish with IngramSpark or Amazon. These both include a service that prints your books when people order them and even ships to buyers for you.

Start-up-y Online Project/App: I know a college student who created a mental health app that not only helped people but also helped pay for his own grad school. Consider this only if you have always dreamed of being an entrepreneur. You must be willing to set accountability tools and devote hundreds of self-directed solo hours to this, with an unclear payoff. Building a successful app is difficult, arduous, and requires coding and other skills. Nonetheless, even if your app fails, the experience is invaluable and can go on your résumé of extracurriculars.

My start-up side project was an attempt to create an online forum in which students could discuss scholarships. The ad revenue was intended to generate micro-scholarships for participants. I built it myself, learning to code along the way, but didn't get many users. Despite my failure, in that my gift to the world did not turn into the new TikTok, this showed that I was someone who takes initiative, exhibits determination, and thinks outside the box. Building something from scratch because you want it to exist is unique! Do not shy away from failing. To be clear, I'm not referring to failing due to a lack of effort in developing a minimum viable version for testing. Ensure that your project reaches a level at which users can interact with it.

EXCEL WITHOUT OVEREXTENDING YOURSELF

Some students stand out by overextending themselves and doing more than four extracurriculars at a time. While this strategy works to get admitted to universities, the risk of burnout is high. A more sustainable way to stand out is to make sure you have the mental bandwidth to excel in the few extracurricular, professional, or academic opportunities you take on.

Notice ways to improve things in your school or extracurriculars—and make the time to work toward that. Take time to listen to people's complaints and think creatively about ways to make your organization, school, employer, or club a little bit more efficient. Thinking actively like this is a highly sought after trait to develop. Proactively seeking out inefficiencies can be your secret strategy to come up with new initiatives to lead. These could be a new volunteer outreach subcommittee or a creative way to fundraise for your club or nonprofit. At your job, you could set up a feedback survey for customers or a better way to automate tasks. You'll have a more substantive way to list your extracurriculars, with a focus on accomplishments, rather than just being a member of several clubs. Also, staff will notice your contributions and likely think of you for opportunities or even awards.

Also, consider making your few extracurriculars very different from each other, as long as they align with a set of interests that make you seem consistent, driven, and focused. The high school student who got into Yale despite having only a total of three extracurriculars arranged for each extracurricular to be very different from the others: one was passion based (drama), another skill based (trivia), and the third was impact based (organizing Special Olympics).

KEEP A LOG THAT DOUBLES AS A KILLER RÉSUMÉ

Keep track of these extracurriculars, your jobs, and your accomplishments within them. I do this by maintaining a very long and detailed résumé that tracks the start and end dates of my extracurriculars, jobs, and volunteer opportunities, four or five bullet points on what I did, and the name of any manager or teammates. This résumé serves as a "master" jumbo résumé for me to pull from to create one-page résumés with three bullet points per role for job or internship applications. I *never* share the jumbo résumé.

Résumés tailored for the position you're applying to perform significantly better than generic résumés. I choose examples to highlight from my jumbo résumé that specifically show why I exceed the job's requirements.

You'll be writing a lot of university applications—so having all your extracurriculars in one place with the highlights of your accomplishments is critical. You'll likely struggle to remember the details of the projects you worked on four semesters ago. Don't accidentally forget an accomplishment and sell yourself short.

A detailed jumbo résumé is also very useful if you end up at a government job. Government jobs often require a very detailed record of your professional experience, including the exact start and end dates and the name of your supervisor.

SPRINKLE IN PRESTIGE

When it comes to extracurricular activities, prestige plays a significant role in setting them apart. Students from high-income backgrounds with strong college support systems are often guided by their families toward higher-prestige opportunities, such as elite music summer camps or exclusive extracurriculars. The most college-savvy parents encourage their children to pursue extracurriculars that are high prestige, yet low time commitment, thereby providing them with an edge in the admissions process.

This leads to yet another system of distortion where high-income students tailor a great-sounding college résumé—and lower-income students would have done just as well if they had the same guidance.

Thus, you should also find and keep track of high-prestige opportunities.

What this looks like:

- Find and apply to prestigious summer camps (like in music, debate, robotics, writing, chess, even politics). These usually have scholarships for low-income students. Camps are typically targeted to high school students but some also exist for college students, taking place in either the summer or right before the semester starts. One of the best ways to find out about the best ones in your region is via instructors.

- Some are free and not very well known:
    - The Summer Program for Applied Rationality and Cognition is a free two week program to help high school students develop quantitative skills and apply them to the world. Apply at https://www.sparc-camp.com/.
    - The Fulbright United Kingdom Summer Institutes are three- to four-week programs for U.S. undergraduate students who have no or very little travel experience outside North America. Participants can explore the UK while experiencing higher education at a UK university. I was put on the reserve list for this during my second year at community college. Get more details at: https://www.fulbright.org.uk/going-to-the-uk/uk-summer-institutes.
    - The French Embassy offers study abroad scholarships specifically for community college students. Check out community-college-specific opportunities at websites like https://ccieworld.org/grants-scholarships/scholarships-for-study-abroad/, which are specific to California community college students. Nonetheless, many of their listed opportunities are not specific to California students.
    - The online Non-Trivial Fellowship helps high school students between the age of 14-20 start an impactful research, policy, or entrepreneurial project. The fellowship includes a $500 scholarship and potentially up to $30,000 in funding. Apply at https://www.non-trivial.org/.

- Entering local, state, and national competitions/awards for whatever skills or hobbies you have (except video games): chess, music, writing, journalism, robotics, etc. Find out about niche competitions from your professors (e.g., for chess opportunities, ask the professor affiliated with the chess club) or search online.

- Harvard alum Lynette used competitions in her college applications. She submitted papers for National History Day (https://nhd.org/en/) after learning about it from a teacher. The projects took a lot of effort, but given the low number of competitors, getting to state level was not too difficult.

- Join the honors program at your school. Consider also any national honors program. However, look for those that offer waivers for membership fees. National honors programs or societies might not make you stand out much since so many students join.

- Seek to volunteer with or join high-prestige teams near you. Does your city's top music conservatory have any programs for high school students? Do you live next to a medical school, Shakespeare festival, research nonprofit, a federal laboratory, an international company's car factory, or anything that is unusual and not found in other cities? Ask around if you can do some free work for them if no student jobs are readily available.

- Work with city or state government or politics. At the lowest, smallest level of political parties, there are often many power vacuums that you could fill. You can similarly participate in local or state government, either as an intern or a volunteer.

- Apply to speak at your city's local TEDx. Subscribe to their newsletter to get alerted when speaker applications open. I spoke about road safety issues in my city, since that is what my volunteer experience focused on. While I did this as an adult, TEDx is open to anyone over eighteen. One of the people in my cohort was a nineteen-year-old college student who spoke about his experience growing up in national parks. The experience doesn't have to be one you directly experienced, either. One of my favorite fellow speakers spoke about her grandmother's experience in the Colombian civil war. If there's any unusual experience or family story, research project, or volunteer experience you want to talk about, TEDx and other similar programs can shine a light on it—and shine a light on you!

Another, more in-depth way to generate prestige is to have an almost unbelievable Grand Project that your extracurriculars or side efforts contribute to throughout your school career. In his book *How to Win at College*, Cal Newport suggests that having a Grand Project should elicit a "Wow!" response when explained to others and should keep you constantly excited and energetic. Ideally, this would align with your deepest desires, like writing long fiction (stories, a screenplay, a novel, etc.) to submit to student competitions, submitting op-eds to local papers until you can work up to a national paper. He notes that you'll need an "anything is possible" mindset and constantly work toward a group of achievable, nonacademic accomplishments that move you closer to your far-off goals.

Grand Projects I've seen firsthand: publishing a book on growing and scaling teams during university, landing a writer gig for an influential journal by freshman year, and launching a software engineering company with friends.

There are tons of other ways to generate prestige. Keep these ideas in mind as you're talking to professors and choosing extracurriculars and academic projects. However, this is less important than a strong foundation: unique extracurriculars and great grades.

FROM ORDINARY TO EXTRAORDINARY: INCORPORATING UNSOLVED PROBLEMS IN YOUR ACADEMIC WORK

I have a friend who was offered one of the oldest and most prestigious scholarships in the world, the Rhodes Scholarship, partly because of my friend's unusual and high-impact focus on existential risks. (Rhodes Scholars receive full funding to study at Oxford in any field of study for two or more years.)

Consider focusing your class essays or even summer internships on pressing problems. Those essays can then double as
samples of your analytical and writing skills to apply for research projects and internships (and later universities and fellowships). By tackling existing open problems, you can make
the essays and reports you're doing for class more unusual,
sophisticated, and distinguished.

The career planning nonprofit 80,000 Hours has a collection
of high-impact and neglected questions for many fields and majors.[9] As an example, within the field of existential risk—that
is, research and advocacy aimed at reducing the chances of a
human-imperiling catastrophe—you could research scenario-planning for engineered pandemics, the runaway greenhouse effect from climate change, or ways to reduce the likelihood of military conflicts between the United States, Russia,
and China.[10] See the Appendix for a fuller list of existential risk–
related ideas.

If you find a topic you really like, you could even start an independent research project for college credit like I did. These are
typically half-credit courses where your professor guides you
through writing a long thesis paper. Ask your favorite professor
how starting one works. The project can sometimes be as creative as a work of visual art, an opera, or a screenplay.

THE MAGIC OF SUMMERS

Most students admitted to selective universities boosted their
resumes by spending their summers doing substantial nonacademic experiences like internships, volunteering, or some
other paid or unpaid unique employment. To me, this was one
of the biggest mindset shifts. I needed my summers to work
more hours at my retail or restaurant employments.

However, you can get the best of both worlds: great experience and pay. The key to getting funded or top summer op-

9   https://80000hours.org/articles/research-questions-by-discipline/.
10   https://80000hours.org/2020/04/longtermist-policy-ideas/.

portunities is to plan early. Starting in August, review summer opportunities weekly. Some of the most exciting opportunities have very early deadlines (January or February) and require similar preparation to university or scholarships applications. Some tech, consulting, and government internships (e.g., NSA, FBI, Department of State) have deadlines as early as September for the following summer. Government internships tend to have very early deadlines because it can take several months to get a security clearance. Paid research internships and programs with generous financial aid also tend to have earlier deadlines.

There are so many types of summer opportunities to consider, like summer research programs and internships in science, arts, media, business, tech companies, or other career paths. Some national institutions offer unusual programs like the National Parks' youth and young adults programs for people between the ages of fifteen and thirty.[11] Also, the Smithsonian Institution, the world's largest museum, education, and research complex, has a large summer internship program in a variety of fields.[12] Your church groups and AmeriCorps are good ideas for impactful summer activities. You can also consider programs where you intern or volunteer abroad.

Summers can also be an opportunity for you to work in a professional job near you. Ask your professors for any firms or organizations that would love some extra help. Check out jobs with local places like news sites, nonprofits, political offices, research institutions, or law firms. Reach out by emailing if you don't see any student jobs available. Some institutions would be glad to have a student help out and would be open to setting something up.

Top places to find internships or summer opportunities, apart from asking professors: your school's job listing site or alumni network, LinkedIn, GlassDoor, Internships.com, Internmatch.com, and specific Google searches. Try using search

---

11   https://www.nps.gov/subjects/youthprograms/jobs-and-internships.htm.
12   https://internships.si.edu/.

terms like "internship + my hometown," "marketing intern-ship near me," "summer student programs," etc.

Make sure you are also checking your state's youth workforce opportunities if you are eligible. I got paired with the local public radio station through a Texas Workforce Development program that was created specifically for lower-income students.

PRIORITIZE YOUR GOALS AND YOURSELF RUTHLESSLY

To prioritize, I set the intention that, for the two years between my first semester of college and the end of my sophomore year, school and extracurricular activities would be my default activities between 9 a.m. and 7 p.m. I filled those hours with a mix of schoolwork, volunteering, paid work, and extracur-riculars, occasionally working late nights when I was waiting tables. This daily 9 a.m. to 7 p.m. schedule felt like an ideal job because I could decide what to work on, focusing on only what was helpful to my goals. I could also schedule breaks based on when I worked best and tailor my schedule to suit me. Essen-tially, I was managing the start-up of me.

For managing my energy, I chose extracurriculars that I was genuinely excited about and where I made good friends. That way, none of them felt like a chore. Seeing firsthand how much a group of dedicated people could achieve expanded my un-derstanding of the world in ways that class lectures could not. I shaped and grew my identity as an advocate and learned about the power I have to make actual changes in my school, work, community, and even the world.

Energy aside, learning to prioritize tasks and manage your time is a crucial skill to develop, though its often not explicit-ly taught. I used Google Calendar to protect me from setting too many commitments. Every time I have a new commitment (like a meeting, volunteer session, tutoring session, or office hour), I immediately put it on my calendar. Adding the event immediately prevents the event from taking up mental space in my head and ensures I don't miss deadlines. I can also easily see if I'm taking on too much on a specific day. This is my cue to either shift things around or consider taking a step back.

Throughout these pages, I emphasize the need for laser focus to make your dreams come true. This focus might mean deprioritizing some things temporarily, but trusting that you'll get bits of your dream life in time. As an example, actively going on dates and finding a partner will be challenging during the semesters you're trying to get into college.

Looking back, I wish I had de-emphasized dating and having a partner those four semesters, partly because I became an entirely different person by the end of this college journey. I took time to develop my own identity as an assertive, determined, and confident person. I raised the standards to which I hold *myself* because I know what I am capable of. You'll change so much as you push yourself, interact with people on missions similar to yours, and find your own success.

Remember that people who you meet during high school or your first few years at your local college are a small percentage of the people you will meet over the course of your life, especially if you move away from your hometown and pursue exciting opportunities. Odds are that your perfect match is someone you haven't yet met.

Additionally, the traits or even things you think you need right now may not even matter to you in the future. One of my dreams used to be to own a Mini Cooper car. Now I dream of living in a walkable community where I never need to own a car again. The person you're dating or the material possessions you desire will likely change, and most importantly, won't define your happiness in the long run. Happiness is about making choices that align with your goals and lead to a fulfilling life.

That said, the long relationship I had during early college worked solely because he was supportive of my goals. He never questioned me putting my schoolwork and dreams first (yay, healthy boundaries). We saw each other two to three times a week depending on my schoolwork and responsibilities load.

Overall, the most important relationship throughout this process is your relationship with yourself: creating and sticking to a study system, tooting your own horn, setting goals, and discarding limiting beliefs can feel scary and difficult. But these are the keys to the car—a surefire way of achieving your goals.

It will be stressful to try to accomplish the same things as higher-income students who have more support, don't need to work, have a functional car, and can easily afford textbooks. Occasionally, I felt overwhelmed and shed tears because it seemed impossible to be a top student with obstacles like unreliable transportation stranding me on the freeway on the way to class.

When times got tough, I always reminded myself of my goal to get into just one of the seventy-five schools. As long as I was in the top 30 percent of my class—a manageable goal—and met the admissions criteria, I was going to get a guaranteed scholarship. Once I was living in a dorm, I wouldn't need to rely on my erratic car and could easily walk to class. Despite the stress and challenges, I kept thinking about my dream of attending a prestigious school, living in a dorm, studying abroad, and having a different, more exciting life.

CHAPTER 6
BUILD A TEAM OF ALLIES

GET HIDDEN OPPORTUNITIES
AND EXCELLENT LETTERS OF
RECOMMENDATION

One common mistake made by students is failing to cultivate **mentor relationships** with their teachers (or professors if you're in college) and counselors. Whenever I ask my more relaxed Ivy League alum friends how they landed a cool research project, internship, or independent study during high school or college, they often credit a teacher or professor who either alerted them to the opportunity or even helped them create it. Taylor, the Princeton alum from Chapter 3, was recommended for a research opportunity at a local university by a high school teacher who was a mentor too. In my own experience, a professor alerted me to an unadvertised volunteer project with the renowned World Bank.

TEACHERS, PROFESSORS, AND MENTORS SUPERCHARGE YOU

Instructors can provide the informal introductions and advice necessary to get selected for major scholarships, competitive programs, dream internships, awards, and more.

I would have never applied for the national Pickering Fellowship that *ended up giving me over $100,000 in scholarships* for both undergraduate and graduate degrees, as well as all-expenses-paid internships and a career serving as a U.S. diplomat. I only applied because a friend and a professor flagged it for me and encouraged me; they believed in me. Your teachers and professors are eager to do the same for you.

For high school students:

Teachers are often incredibly passionate about supporting their students, which is what drives them in their profession. I have a friend who had a high school teacher that went above and beyond by finding small essay contests for students to apply to, which helped boost their résumé's prestige. This teacher even offered extra credit for participating. Additionally, this same friend had another teacher who took the time to explain the intricacies of AP class GPA calculations.

Another inspiring story involves my friend named Ronan. Initially, Ronan was not considered "college track," but everything changed when his teacher and guidance counselor encouraged him to skip class in order to fill out a multi-scholarship application. Surprisingly, his teachers even approved of this! Ronan wrote a few short essays, submitted the application, and then completely forgot about it.

Months later, Ronan received incredible news – he was awarded a full college scholarship, including living expenses, from a private foundation. The financial support he received was on par with the wages he would have earned as a gas station attendant, the job he had been considering. This unexpected turn of events prompted Ronan to figure out how to apply for college. Despite initially being ineligible for university admission due to having dropped out of high school years earlier, Ronan managed to secure admission to his local university through a special process. He excelled academically, which eventually led to his acceptance into Yale Law School, the most prestigious law school globally.

Ronan's story is a testament to the transformative power of dedicated teachers.

For college students:

Professors are invaluable resources, partly due to the rigorous process of becoming one in America. With limited academic job opportunities and a large number of PhD graduates each year, those who secure professor roles are truly exceptional. Even small rural schools require qualifications on par with Ivy League universities, which is why professors often hail from different regions. As a result, their connections and networks extend far beyond their local areas. (Remember my Virginia professor who introduced me to my future nonprofit internship in my Texas hometown, 2,000 miles away?)

Moreover, professors can also play a vital role in guiding you through the complex and competitive American college system. Being the first in my family to graduate from a U.S. college, receiving tailored guidance from knowledgeable PhD graduates who understand the competitive university application process made a huge difference.

Research indicates that high-income students receive support from family and friends throughout their university journey, while low-income students often lack such mentorship. This lack of guidance contributes to the challenges and higher dropout rates experienced by low-income students.

Professors serve as the ultimate equalizers, helping level the playing field. University life has its own unwritten rules and strategies for success. While this book is a valuable resource, there is still much to learn, and time is limited.

Instructors can become like your team of **advisers**, similar to the president's cabinet of advisers. They can help you make important decisions about which internships to pursue and accept, which majors or minors to consider, which classes to take, which summer programs to apply to, and which post-graduate opportunities to pursue. My professor even helped me prep for the Pickering Fellowship finalist interviews by letting me ask him questions for over an hour about all my foreign policy knowledge gaps. While other students may have college-educated family members to turn to for advice, you have the next best thing: experts in their fields who have experience helping many students succeed.

Don't be afraid to reach out to instructors for help. I often go back to campus to thank my professors for the tremendous impact they had on my life, including writing and submitting over fifteen recommendation letters for me and mentoring me. They always express how glad they are to have helped me achieve my dreams, which is why they pursued teaching in the first place: to help students like me and you.

HOW TO DEVELOP MENTORSHIPS WITH TEACHERS OR PROFESSORS

Developing relationships with instructors is similar to making friends. The relationships have to develop naturally, but there are ways to increase the likelihood of forming a mentorship:

1. Be engaged in class. While less obvious than one-on-one time, this sets a good impression of who you are. Being engaged means never missing class, not being late to class, speaking up with insightful questions, and answering the instructor's questions to show that you did do the reading. As someone who was shy in school, I found answering questions in front of everyone difficult, but I tried to do it at least once a class or every other class. Speaking up in class is an important habit—imagine how hard it is, for a professor, to address a class full of potatoes who nev-

er respond. Make eye contact with your professor when they are speaking, if you can; it's common courtesy, easy to do, and this is something you will be grateful for when it's your turn to speak to a group. Some instructors even keep a tally of how often students speak up in class and incorporate this into the final grade.

- A mentor of mine who became CEO of a well-known institution early in their career credits their success to speaking up with something insightful at least once in every single meeting.

2. After class or during any one-on-one time, be open about your goals and struggles. If your instructor doesn't know that you're a lower-income student aiming to get into top schools, they can't give you personalized advice and recommendations. You can do this by mentioning why you chose the ten universities (because your income qualifies for their promise), why you're not considering music/policy/math summer programs (no financial aid), or noting opportunities you used that are only for lower-income students (Pell Grant, state youth workforce programs, etc.). I know that you might usually prefer to hide these markers of low- and middle-income status, but don't hide it from professors. If you're closer to middle income than low income (as in the $70,000 to $100,000 range), your big struggle might look like aiming to reinvent yourself after a less-than-stellar high school experience and aiming to get admitted to the top universities with the financial aid you need. You'll stand out for working hard toward specific and ambitious goals.

3. Keep in touch with the instructors you like even after your class with them ends. Send them an email or pop into their office or classroom once or twice a semester, updating them with what summer internships or volunteer opportunities you're considering, any nonprofit or school clubs you're now involved with, or just asking how they are doing.

4. *For college students only:* Go to office hours. Office hours are a great time to get the professor's feedback on essay thesis ideas, supportive evidence for essays, and clarification on any topics you didn't fully understand from class or homework. This is also a chance to introduce yourself more fully—tell your professor about your major, why you chose their class, what your dreams/goals are, then ask your professor about their story. As your relationship with the professor grows, gradually transition the conversation to academic advice. Ask them to flag for you any fellowships, scholarships, internships, or job openings in your major (if their class relates to your major). They might have a ready-made list, or they will keep you in mind if they hear of opportunities.

- On the other hand: DON'T go to office hours to ask for coursework help unless you've done the required reading and prep up to that day of class. Their time is as valuable as yours, and you both will get far more out of the moments you spend together if you prepare. You don't want to make the professor reteach you what you should have learned from class or the reading. Coming in unprepared could make a bad impression, something you don't want to risk.

You're building a network of professionals who can provide last-minute introductions and share exciting opportunities.

Don't feel weird about asking instructors for guidance and support even after you've completed their class. Remember that your success is also your school's success and even your instructors' success! Both high schools and colleges highlight student success stories (like your future story) to show other students what they're capable of *and* to showcase the school's greatness. Community colleges especially love to advertise when students transfer to four-year universities, particularly selective ones!

Aim to have an active mentorship relationship with **three** instructors throughout your time in school leading up to when you apply for universities. Most universities require two or three letters of recommendation.

If you find that the instructor you're interested in doesn't seem open or available to a mentorship-type relationship, it could be because they are too busy with other academic duties, or, if you're in college, they may simply prefer to focus on research rather than teaching. It's also possible that they are not fans of you specifically, although this is less likely. You will have at least forty teachers over the course of college, so move on to another option.

College students: Adjunct professors may be less available for mentoring because they're at the university for a shorter time or have a separate full-time job. Established permanent professors (like assistant professors or associate professors) are generally more available for mentoring.

You can help repay your supportive instructors back by nominating them for "instructor of the year" types of awards. In the justification, describe in detail their guidance, support, and devotion to students like you. I have personally nominated multiple instructors, and some of them have won!

DIVERSIFYING YOUR TEAM OF ALLIES: UNIVERSITY STAFF, MANAGERS, AND BOSSES

Instructors aren't the only allies in your team of advisers. Your team of advisers can also consist of other staff with whom you work closely because of your extracurriculars. You'll likely know when the relationship is right for mentoring—as with building friendships, there is a natural gravitation factor. If you are doing your work and using the strategies in this book, you'll likely have multiple people who mentor you.

Some might even come out of the woodwork in ways you didn't realize they could. When I was a semifinalist for a fully funded United Kingdom summer program with Fulbright, two community college staff members from the Student Leadership and Campus Life Department were my biggest allies. These two, whom I met because of my work as a student senator, taught me critical strategies for interviewing for competitive programs (e.g., having two or three questions prepared beforehand to ask the interviewers). These two staff members worked closely and long enough with me that they also could have written me letters of recommendation, even though they were never my formal instructors or supervisors. They also flagged opportunities that I wouldn't have otherwise thought of and encouraged me when I didn't get selected for that Fulbright summer program.

Reach out to your school's counselors and student life staff. Let them know about your goals and ask for any helpful resources. A friend of mine found out about a fully funded tour of a top university via her guidance counselor! If you're nervous about admissions interviews, ask them about coaching. Even if they don't offer coaching, they might know someone who does.

In some cases, your managers, bosses, or colleagues at your internship, volunteer work, or professional experience can become mentors and advisers for you. You'll likely naturally develop a professional relationship with your managers or bosses, due to working with them for so long. You can turn this into more of a mentorship relationship by asking for their advice and guidance on academic and greater career matters. Often, your colleagues or higher-ups will have experience with the university system, a strong professional network, tips on getting other internships in the field, and can give you specific feedback on how to be a better intern, employee, or researcher.

One of your letters of recommendation for university admissions can stem from a professional experience, so developing a mentorship relationship will make that letter more powerful and authentic. Make sure to keep in touch with them!

LEVERAGING YOUR NETWORK: ASK FOR HELP WITHOUT FEELING AWKWARD

Have you ever asked a friend for help? Asking for help typically doesn't feel awkward if you've kept in touch with that friend, told that friend in advance that you might someday reach out to them for support, and kept the favor small.

The same thing applies with your instructors, school staff, and professional colleagues. You may need to ask for favors such as writing a letter of recommendation, introducing you to potential internships, or being a reference for job applications. The trick to asking for help without feeling awkward is in what you do *before* you need the help.

Do the following right now:

1. Make a Google Doc spreadsheet (or Evernote, Notion, or some other note management software you already depend on) that lists the name of the professors, managers, bosses, and professionals with whom you would like to keep in touch and/or are developing mentorship relationships with.

2. Make a column called "Date Last Contacted."

3. Add the last time you reached out to them. A month is fine. You'll want to ensure to reach out if three or four months have passed since your last contact. Contact can be an email checking in, popping into their classroom or office, or chatting with them at some mutual event.

    a. *College students:* Often, professors keep office hours open to all students, not just students in a course with them.

4. Create a "Notes" column to record important information about your mentors. This can include their advice that you plan to implement and report back to them, potential introductions they offered to make for you, or any issues where you could provide assistance. Add life details like birthdays, interests, family details, or hobbies, like bubble wrap popping. By maintaining these notes, you can easily stay in touch and periodically check in with your mentors. They will appreciate seeing that you take their advice seriously when you show how you acted upon it later. Additionally, sharing relevant news or particularly satisfying bubble wrap is a great way to reconnect.

5. Add another column called "To Do," where you note any items that you told the contact that you would send them.

Make it easy to access this document by "starring" it or adding it to your bookmarks bar. Adding to this spreadsheet should be as easy and frictionless as possible, so that you use it consistently.

HOW TO CONFIRM WHETHER YOU'VE MADE A GOOD IMPRESSION

Keep in mind, your instructors and your contacts are much more likely to help if you made an excellent impression on them. Writing you a letter of recommendation, introducing you to a potential employer, and putting in a good word for you is your contact using their social capital on you. If there's any reason to think you might not be a stellar intern for your new team, your contact's relationship with that team will suffer because your contact had put in a good word for you. Make a good impression by doing a good job at the projects you are juggling and treating others well.

A test to know whether you're making a good impression can also be to ask your contact for ways to improve—for example, as a student academically in their class, as a student involved in extracurriculars, and as a potential employee during interviews. Any way that you can invite feedback can help you improve and also show that you're self-aware. Take any feedback with grace, make no excuses, and thank them.

If you know you've made a good impression on the professor or contact, either because they commend your work in class, have told you that your future is promising, or any other sign, ask them if they'd be willing to send out letters of recommendation for you next year when you apply for schools. Aim to only ask those who have shown a particularly strong belief in your skills and future.

CHAPTER 7
BE UNSTOPPABLE

MAKE YOUR SUCCESS INEVITABLE

A close friend of mine, Ruby, dropped out of college due to unexpected medical bills that she couldn't afford. Ruby was in student government and on track to graduate with honors, thanks to her impressive academic record and enviable extracurriculars. She inspired me to see myself as a leader. It was heartbreaking to see such a talented and capable individual forced to leave school like this.

DEFEATING THE MOST PROBABLE ROADBLOCKS

With sadness, I have seen many other brilliant friends drop out due to similar challenges. This made me realize how important it is to *anticipate roadblocks* and *build up your defenses against the most common obstacles*. Some of the top reasons students nationwide drop out include financial constraints, school costs, and personal and family situations.[13] As you consider these, bear in mind: life events don't just happen to "some" people, nor do they happen to "other people," they happen to *everyone*. When (not if) they happen to you, remember that you are in the driver's seat, and you are unstoppable.

The top reasons I've seen lower-income students drop out are as follows:

1. Family financial constraints
2. Medical bills
3. Reduction in flexibility due to the wrong kinds of commitments

Family Financial Constraints

When you have younger siblings or very elderly or disabled family members, focusing on yourself for several semesters can seem impossible or selfish. You are deliberately lowering the number of hours you work (and thus, money you bring home) to build up your extracurriculars. However, focusing on

13   https://www.petersons.com/blog/top-11-reasons-why-college-students-drop-out-dont-let-it-happen-to-you/.

your academics and schools for those semesters will significantly increase your chances of doubling or tripling your income in the future. The average young college graduate's salary is $59,600 a year (source: National Center for Education Statistics, 2023). You will likely be able to make more money than that, from the jump, since you'll be an above-average student who built strong professional experience and networks during your time in school.

Think of these semesters as an investment in your family. This mindset might help as you spend your hard-earned money on college costs (textbooks, gas money, application fees). Education is the main route out of poverty in America. This is your and your family's way of not getting stuck.

Action steps:

- *Prioritize applying for on-campus jobs* that pay better than minimum wage and that will double as professional experience. Some of these jobs can also double as study time; some could provide you with connections for your future career. On-campus jobs are competitive, so continue to apply throughout the semester, even if you've been turned down. Some research or professional jobs related to your major (like computer science or data analysis) pay significantly above minimum wage.

    - Student jobs at my university library paid well and provided a lot of study time. I was a "building monitor" for my department. Being tethered to a quiet reception desk, and other low-profile high-downtime job sites, are ideal environments for studying.

    - My friend and roommate Marjie did work-study as a college recruiter, which also cut down on her time commuting around town. This recruiter role's access to school news also made other college activities easier such as writing for the school paper.

    - My friend Kat worked as a computer lab tech, a job with ample downtime to study and build soft skills (customer service, etc.). Some student coworkers even advanced to lab manager positions, improving their résumés and earning higher pay.

- Casey and I met when we were both student technicians for Yale's IT services. Casey got promoted and ended up working there right after undergrad!

- *Apply every week to smaller scholarships* (less than $3,000) to keep you afloat! After your tuition and school fees are covered, the scholarships go to you as cash. You can apply for scholarships at all stages, before and during college. Because of your extracurriculars, you'll be an excellent candidate for local scholarships. On page 127, you'll find my system for winning these scholarships.

Also remember that you automatically get the **US government's $6,495 Pell Grant** each year if you apply on time and qualify as a low-income student in good academic standing. This can cover the average community college ($5,100 a year)—and the extra grant funds go straight to your bank account. Make sure to spend it wisely (textbooks and bills) and save some for emergencies like car trouble and any future school costs not covered by scholarships.

You may also qualify for additional grants without even applying. Because I maintained a high GPA at my community college and was a Pell Grant recipient, Texas deposited a $1,000 grant into my bank account. I was so confused, I called my community college to find out whether this was an error.

Medical Bills

You *need* health insurance. Even if you're young and healthy. In America, a single visit to the emergency room without insurance costs an average of $2,200. If you get into a car crash or get a serious illness, you could owe hundreds of thousands of dollars. You might have to take a semester off to figure out how to handle the debt and work to pay it off.

You qualify to stay on your parent's health insurance until you're *twenty-six*. If they don't have health insurance, apply for Medicaid. If you don't qualify, review your options on your state's online health insurance marketplace and your college's health insurance plan.

In some cases, you can ask that the school consider the health insurance plan in your cost of college so that you can use scholarships toward the cost.

Reduction in Flexibility Due to the Wrong Kinds of Commitments

Elon Musk once tried to live on a dollar's worth of food per day to ensure that he would be able to survive through any periods of hardships while getting his start-up off the ground. He wanted to see how flexible his income level could be. He lived in a small, dingy apartment and ate bulk grocery food like hot dogs, oranges, and pasta.

I am in no way recommending that you do this. But there is something to be said about protecting your time and freedom by keeping your expenses low.

Avoid signing up for expensive commitments like car loans, expensive apartment leases, or luxury items. Any expenses you lock yourself into at this point will cost you too many hours of your precious time during semesters.

As an example, a $20,000 car loan (the cheapest new-car price today) will cost you $555 a month with a thirty-six months interest-free loan. If you get paid $10 an hour, you've just signed away fifty-five hours a month (roughly fourteen hours a week, two hours of every single day) solely to owning this car.

The car alone is over a third of the forty hours a week that you need to devote to academics and extracurriculars. You'll need to work even more hours to pay for gas and car insurance.

Also, you'll have to continue spending fourteen hours a week to pay for this car even after you move to a faraway university where you likely won't need a car. Typically, dorm life means you can walk to class, work, and your extracurriculars; campuses are designed to be walkable.

My strategy: in high school and college, I had a $3,000 car that the dealer let me pay off in installments. Looking back, I probably should have spent $4,000 to $5,000 for a car that was more dependable. There's no real need to spend much more than that.

Nowadays, even after seven years in a well-paid professional career, I still chose to drive a Toyota Matrix that I bought for under $7,000 when it was over ten years old. While I live car-free in a walkable city, I drove this affordable hatchback across the country and even brought it with me on a diplomatic assignment in Egypt. Before buying the Toyota Matrix, I invested $99 in a prepurchase inspection from a mechanic to make sure the car was in great condition; the dealer fixed about $600 worth of small issues that the mechanic found.

On that same note, be open to spending money on things that save you time or keep you safe. Alexa, who got into UC Berkeley after community college, used to spend over three hours on buses daily, sometimes walking through unsafe areas late at night. Looking back, she notes the occasional Uber or Lyft would have been well worth it, especially if she'd used the extra time productively.

Pets can also be an issue if you get them during college rather than after college, as the experience of Aria in Chapter 3 illustrated. If you have a pet, make sure you know who can take care of your pet when you are away at university. Dorms do not allow pets.

DON'T LET YOUR JOB OWN YOU

Apart from making sure you don't *need* a lot of hours at your job by keeping your expenses and financial commitments low, you might also find yourself having to push back at your workplace to ensure your academics don't suffer.

Unfortunately, America doesn't offer a lot of protections for minimum wage workers. In retail, grocery stores, and restaurants, you often don't get to know your shift more than a week in advance, making planning your week difficult. If you find that your employer isn't holding up their end of the bargain to avoid scheduling you for night shifts on weeknights or is getting upset at you for not volunteering for last-minute shifts, start looking for another job as soon as possible. You should probably always be looking out for job openings if your main job(s) aren't giving you professional experience, an unusually high wage, or some other unusual benefit.

Throughout my time in college, I rarely had fewer than two jobs. You also might find yourself having to hold down two or three jobs, primarily because some jobs limit the number of hours they give employees. I've had retail jobs that wouldn't give me more than 8-10 hours a week of work. If you have employers who respect your time outside of work and are predictable and dependable, you should be able to juggle two or three jobs about as easily as handling one job. Put them in your calendar alongside your other responsibilities, and do not let the jobs take priority.

If possible, keep some "FU" money in a savings account to ensure you never feel stuck in a specific job. I have been using Ally Bank, an online-only bank, that pays *me* a high-interest rate for keeping my money in its savings and checking accounts. Seeing that your saved money is earning you money (as of early 2023, Ally is giving out a 3.85 percent interest rate on savings accounts) encouraged me to set up a habit of saving.

SURROUND YOURSELF WITH INSPIRING PEOPLE

At student senate, I met people who were good at launching big projects. In debate, I met people who had mastered the art of communication, after years of work. Through volunteering with low-income communities, I met passionate advocates who had dedicated their lives to social impact.

As I spent more time with these individuals, my friend group shifted, and I felt less like the odd one out. I met people who were very social-impact motivated, like me. As a side perk, I also started to hear about new nonprofits, fellowships, jobs, and projects because of being plugged into a network of people who also cared about excelling.

As the saying goes, "You are the average of the five people you spend the most time with." Therefore, it's crucial to surround yourself with individuals who inspire and motivate you, and help you feel supported and connected.

GET SMALL SCHOLARSHIPS FOR FAST CASH

Scholarships can help with more than just tuition; scholarships can help pay for books and living expenses too.

College students: If you're short on money for rent, food, bus fare, car repairs, tuition, or books, your school probably has an emergency fund and other resources like food pantries. Don't hesitate to seek support if you are struggling to meet basic needs. If you still need help and are pursuing a degree in a STEM field, check out LastMile-ed.org, a first-come first-served scholarship fund based on need, not on academics. The fund offers emergency grants up to $599 and larger grants for college juniors and seniors.

Whether in high school or college, apply often for small scholarships to cover financial gaps. Add any wins to your résumé.

Optimal strategy for small scholarships:

1. Search for scholarships that fewer students know about or qualify for. Start with your school's list of scholarships.

2. Many scholarship applications require an essay that tells your story. Draft one high-quality, resonant, and unusual essay. Make it personal, not a list of accomplishments. Have your professors and mentors review it. Reuse this essay for all your scholarship applications.

   a. For each scholarship application, tweak your essay. Save all versions, as well any cover letters and university admissions essays before you submit them. You can reuse these, since scholarships typically ask for similar essay prompts or cover letters.

3. Use your jumbo, very detailed résumé to copy and paste your accomplishments into your scholarship applications.

4. Apply to as many small scholarships as possible, as quickly as possible. You'll improve and send out great applications more quickly over time. Applications will feel easier!

5. Set a weekly time for applying for scholarships. I recommend one or two hours on Saturday afternoons. Use Focusmate to pre-commit to fifty-minute sessions—applying to small scholarships is something you might not look forward to because of how many rejections you can expect.

In the book *The Scholarship System*, author Jocelyn Paonita, lists other places to search for not-so-famous scholarships:

1. **Academic Counselors.** Your high school guidance counselor and college financial-aid counselor likely have a collection of scholarships that are less well-known and only target students in your city. Your department or major's counselor might have an even more curated list.

2. **Scholarship websites with large databases, primarily Fastweb.com and Collegeboard.com.** Beware of unreputable websites that promise random scholarships in exchange for your email—these websites are likely spam.

3. **Googling very specific search terms.** Search for combinations of your hobbies/extracurriculars/major plus the term "scholarship" or "cash award." For example, if you're a chess club member, type in "chess" and "scholarship." You might also find more specific scholarships by typing in "chess" and another more specific thing about yourself, like "woman," "first generation," "low income," "restaurant worker," or "Texas." To explore even further, you could replace "scholarship" with "foundation" or "organization" to see if any nonprofits offer scholarships on their websites.

   a. Alexa from Chapter 3 had much success with this by finding tailored scholarships while *also* optimizing for fields that have funding. For example, *women* (cuts 50 percent of population out) in *tech* (a field with a lot of funding) or *women* in *privacy and cybersecurity* (more specialized, also considerable funding).

4. **Social media sites.** Twitter is likely the easiest network to search.

5. **Local banks, credit unions, or other local companies' websites.** While at community college, I got a $500 scholarship from my local credit union, even though I wasn't a member.

6. **Books, particularly College Board's yearly *The Ultimate Scholarship Book*.** You can find some great scholarship books at the library.

If you have a big weakness in your application (e.g., low high school grades, no extracurriculars, etc.), be open about why that is. Students don't need perfect grades or amazing extracurriculars to get smaller scholarships, but show them that you're doing your best and you're on a good trajectory.

Other ways to stand out: don't be afraid to reach out with a question about the scholarship or a thank-you note to the folks staffing the scholarship program. You can find the people by either searching on LinkedIn or looking through the scholarship's information page.

CHAPTER 8

APPLY TO TOP UNIVERSITIES LIKE A PRO

KNOW WHAT MAKES YOU
STAND OUT—AND USE IT

Once you have two to four strong high school or college semesters on your résumé, **apply to top universities**. Start working on your applications two or three months before the deadlines. I recommend setting aside three hours a week for this on your calendar.

Overall, universities will usually require all or most of the following:

- *Application*: Give yourself time to find out what materials the application requires, so that you can collect them. You may need tax forms and other proofs of financials, among other materials.

- *Application essay*
  - Plus supplementary essays

- *Transcripts* from high school and college (often less than $40 to send out to multiple schools, free if the schools allow electronic transcripts)

- *Standardized test scores*: SATs or ACTs (the $55 to $85 test fees are waived if you're a high school junior or senior on the federal reduced-price or free lunch program)

- *FAFSA* (the federal government's Free Application for *Federal Student Aid*)

- *The CSS Profile*: a separate, more in-depth financial aid application (The CSS Profile is free for domestic undergraduate students whose family income is up to $100,000. Otherwise, the fee is $25 with $16 for additional reports.)

- *Application fee* charged by the university itself. Most universities use the Common App, which provides application fee waivers if you are eligible for a Pell Grant, the federal free or reduced-price lunch program, or an SAT or ACT fee waiver.

The spreadsheet you made with your list of target universities should have a list of deadlines and any additional requirements.

While a lot of schools waive the fee to send your transcripts to universities, some may not. Preparing for the cost of applying to colleges required a mental shift for me. The idea of spending hundreds of dollars on sending transcripts and standardized tests with no guarantee of getting accepted was daunting. But I knew I had to trust the process and trust myself. I did extensive research to identify schools with easier acceptance rates and viewed my part-time job as a way to cover college application expenses.

> Despite the initial discomfort of spending the money, the $200 I invested in transcripts and test fees allowed me to compare scholarship offers ranging from $10,000 to over $50,000 a year. That's a return on investment I couldn't have achieved otherwise.

If I had limited my university applications to a smaller list of only those schools I thought I would get into, I would never have gotten into Yale! Don't be tempted to shorten your list of universities just to avoid additional essay drafting or save money on sending transcripts and test fees.

Since you're only choosing schools that offer you automatic financial aid, every additional school greatly increases your chances of receiving a nearly-full scholarship. Your success greatly depends on your acceptance alone. Unfortunately, university admissions are very unpredictable and what your nearly-full scholarship hinges on.

If you're still feeling uneasy about the costs, ask a trusted teacher, professor, or counselor to ensure you're on the right track for top schools.

> *Transfer students:* Transfer student acceptance rates are even more unpredictable and fluctuate. Acceptance rates can provide a general sense of a school's competitiveness, but those rates are often based on *freshman-year* applications. The number of available positions for transfer students can greatly vary each year. The number of slots depends on how

> many students decide to leave the school and how many new students apply to transfer in. This can sometimes mean that, if even a few dozen more students apply one year, the acceptance rate becomes harder.

Beyond a certain level of competitiveness—particularly with acceptance rates below 15 percent—getting accepted can also seem like luck. When I applied to Harvard, Yale, Columbia, and Princeton for graduate school, I was only accepted to Yale and Columbia, while a friend with *more* credentials was accepted to Harvard and Princeton. The Princeton program was particularly difficult to get into because every student accepted gets awarded a full scholarship. She got into the toughest of the programs but not into Columbia, which arguably had the easiest acceptance rate of the four universities.

These four programs (Harvard, Yale, Columbia, and Princeton) had similarly tough acceptance rates, and I had no way of knowing which program would accept me. Saving time and dollars on applications can seem appealing, but it could be the very thing that prevents you from receiving a $120,000+ scholarship to an Ivy League school.

Do not make the same mistake that a lot of low-income students make: not applying for the very selective schools.

Acceptable reasons to not apply to a selective school:

- The school lacks your major or any field you're interested in.
- The university is only for women and non-binary folks, and you're neither.
- You're allergic to the sun and the university is in a very sunny state (however, I know someone who did this, so it might not actually be an acceptable reason).

Unacceptable reasons to not apply to a selective school:

- You don't think you'll get in
- Time

- ▪ Cost

I didn't want to apply to all sixteen of the grad school pro-grams I applied to. It seemed wasteful to pay that multi-school cost when I knew that I would attend only one school. I did it anyway because my fellowship required me to attend a school on their list of top schools. Solely because of that requirement, I applied to every school on their list. I never actually expected to get into Yale. In an effort to not waste my time, I would have missed out on attending my dream school.

> Confidence is a key divider between outcomes for low- and high-income students. Applying to top schools demands self-assurance, something that might not have been nurtured in lower-income students. Research has revealed that only students from higher-income households tend to apply to these universities, even more frequently than students with higher grades and scores but from lower-income households.

Bottom line: don't shy away from selective schools just be-cause of their perceived competitiveness. Three reasons why:

1. You have done everything that high-income students have done to be competitive, yet you did it with obstacles against you. Just like the unicorn you are.
2. University admissions officers take into consideration the obstacles you faced and can see your unicorn-ness.
3. You can't tell how rare and special you and your efforts are to universities because you and what's normal to you are all you've ever known. Typical life of a unicorn.

Invest the time and money into your applications, and cast a wide net!

COLLEGE APPLICATIONS: A TIMELINE THAT WORKS BECAUSE IT WINS

Now (the earlier the better):

- Research the list of full-need-met universities and select fifteen to twenty of those universities. These are where you will apply.
    - Of these fifteen to twenty, select four you are most excited about that have easier acceptance rates. These are the first four you'll send your SAT/ACT scores to directly upon taking those tests.
    - Build a spreadsheet of universities that includes relevant deadlines and any unusual requirements.
    - Highlight if the university has earlier deadlines for transfer students or offers early decision for transfer students (like University of Chicago).

- Sign up for the SAT or ACT tests.
    - Take the test early so you can retake it if you need to. Budget for two tries, as you are likely to get better and you can use either.
    - Have your list of four universities on hand when registering for the SAT or ACT. They allow you to send scores to four universities for free, but only at registration.
    - Fees are waived if you are currently a high school junior or senior on federal reduced-price lunch.

- *High school juniors from families earning less than $65,000 per year for a family of four:* Apply for Questbridge's College Prep Scholars Program. This is the most well-known and prestigious college applications support program for high school students at this income level. It boosts your résumé, walks you through competitive college applications, and gives you exclusive access to additional scholarship opportunities, summer program scholarships, personalized essay feedback, access to college fairs, and other specialized resources.

During Upcoming Summer/Winter Breaks:

- Take the SAT or ACT.

The Year Before You Begin University:

February/March:

- Finalize your target list of schools.
- Very important: Fill out financial aid applications for the following academic year. This means the U.S. government's FAFSA and the CSS Profile. Request a waiver for the CSS Profile fees. Send the CSS Profile to your target schools.
    - Filling out the FAFSA and CSS Profile on time is one of the key requirements for some schools. For example, Tulane University's website states that their "no loan" tuition for families making under $75,000 is contingent on completing the FAFSA and CSS Profile by February 15.

June/July:

- Start drafting essays for college applications.
- Consider reaching out to specific professors within each school or alumni to learn more about the programs to which you're applying. Some universities allow you to note in your application that you spoke with alumni or professors.
- Draft a clear list of your accomplishments to give to people who will write recommendation letters about you.
- Ask for letters of recommendation from professors, coaches, or employers.
- *For transfer students:* reach out to transfer admissions counselors to learn more about the program/process.

Ideally, ask for fifteen-minute phone calls to ask any school-specific questions and have a contact in case of any processing issues (e.g., the school didn't get a transcript).

August/September:

- Continue drafting essays for college applications. Have several professors and mentors give you feedback on your essay.

- Request an electronic copy of your transcripts to easily attach it to college applications.

- Attend any college fairs where admissions counselors travel to your area. Talking with admissions counselors can give you someone to contact if any issues with the application process come up and put a face to a name for your application.

- Finalize letters of recommendation.

October/November:

- Send official transcripts to the universities.

- Submit applications.

- Check whether recommendation letters are submitted. Follow up with letter writers if needed.

- Double check applications to make sure universities received all items.

December/January:

- Continue finalizing and submitting college applications.

- Follow up with universities if needed.

SAT / ACT STANDARDIZED TESTS

High scores depend on ruthless accounting of your shortcomings based on practice tests. Take practice tests online and answer a few practice questions every single day.

Zero in on any questions you get wrong to ensure you know exactly what skills you need to improve. I recommend the free study strategy for SAT and ACT tests from PrepScholar.com[14].

Have four of your target universities ready by the day you register for the SAT or ACT. The ACT and SAT allow you to send your scores officially to four schools for no additional fee, though you have to list these schools when you register for the test or before you take the test.

The SAT charges $12 to send your official scores to additional schools; the ACT charges $16. If you qualify for a fee waiver, you can send the scores to as many schools as you like for free.

For fee waivers, sign up for the ACT or SAT before you graduate from high school. If you qualify for free and reduced-price lunch in school or are near the poverty line, you can qualify for a fee waiver for the SAT ($60) or the ACT ($60 to $85), but you must still be in your junior or senior year of high school.

Keep track of which schools accept unofficial test scores! You can always send those for free. Some schools may accept an unofficial exam report instead. To create an unofficial report, log into the SAT or ACT website, see the report of your exam(s), and select "Print" followed by "Save to PDF." You can send this to universities as needed.

Retake SAT or ACT tests if you didn't get a high score. SAT and ACT test scores are more a product of study time and preparation, rather than intelligence. I ended up taking the ACT twice until I got a competitive score; I had to pay out of pocket, but this was worth it.

Alternatively, you could only consider schools that don't require SAT or ACT if you find that you didn't do well on the test despite studying or want to skip standardized testing altogether. Your list of schools will be more limited,

---

14 https://blog.prepscholar.com/how-to-get-a-perfect-act-score-by-a-36-full-scorer.

but universities are trending toward making these tests optional.

WRITE A COMPELLING ESSAY

The college application essay holds *a lot* of weight in your college application. The essay alone is probably as important as your GPA, and it can even make up for a less-than-ideal GPA.

Do *not* make your essay a list of your accomplishments, nor should you try to make your essay another way to make your list of extracurriculars stand out. Your essay is the only place to show that you're a deep thinker, creative, and have a unique personality. Look up some essay examples online to get a sense of how personal they can be.

My favorite guide for writing a great college application is from Harvard's Summer School: https://summer.harvard.edu/blog/12-strategies-to-writing-the-perfect-college-essay/.

- Be authentic. Don't write in formal or "flowery" language that no one would use in conversation. Write about a topic that reveals a lot about who you are, what drives you, and/or any personal situations or childhood background. If your essay is so personal that you'd be uncomfortable with friends or acquaintances reading it, you're probably on the right track.

- Have an attention-grabbing first sentence or paragraph.

- Focus on deeper themes, like realizations you've come to in life or personal internal growth.

- Show, don't tell (this one is trickier, and I recommend asking professors if you have successfully achieved this). Provide anecdotes to make your essay feel engaging.

- Be unique: a lot of students write about sports-related obstacles or success, volunteering, immigration stories, moving, a significant personal achievement, or overcoming obstacles. Feel free to use these but make sure the deeper emotional aspect is at the forefront.

Casey from Chapter 3, who applied to several Ivy League schools, was accepted to Princeton and Yale with a quirky, fun essay but rejected by Harvard, where he had submitted a more standard, accomplishment-focused essay. His applications to the Ivy League schools were otherwise very similar, but he switched between submitting the two types of essays based on the specific essay prompt given by each school.

As an example of a successful essay, see Appendix D for one of Lynette's Harvard admissions essays. She's not rehashing her résumé. She's adding color and an emotional story behind one of her résumé feats.

Moral of the story: Even top-performing students can be rejected by Ivy League schools, and essays can make a huge difference.

FIND YOUR UNIQUE STORY

Reflecting on your life can reveal powerful stories to tell in your essays - but it requires deep self-examination. Keep in mind that you're already a very unusual and unique candidate because your income is near or below the US median income ($70,000). The tricky part is choosing what part of your lived experience to highlight. You've likely mostly been exposed to people whose lives are similar to yours, so you might not feel as though you've gone through anything unusual.

Below are some questions to guide you in mining your memories, background, and inner landscape. These prompts help unpack the moments and relationships that influenced your path. The goal is not to dwell on adversity, but to reflect on the growth, insights, and strengths forged through your lived experiences.

As you explore each question, focus on any vivid memories, emotions, or lessons learned. Look for the stories that give genuine insight into your character. The unique circumstances you navigate make you who you are - and that is what colleges want to see.

1. Did you ever feel a lack of resources, support or guidance that forced you to find your own way? What did you learn from this self-reliance?

2. Have you overcome a health challenge? How did that experience shape your strengths and strategies?

3. Did you grow up with different customs, family structures or beliefs than peers? How did navigating those differences impact you?

4. Have you ever felt excluded, misunderstood or silenced? What gave you courage and voice during those times?

5. Have you faced economic hardship? What lessons did you learn from struggling to make ends meet?

6. Have you lost a loved one or friend? How did you keep their memory and influence alive?

7. Did you take on mature responsibilities at a young age, like caring for siblings, filling parental roles, or managing a household? What inner strength and empathy did you gain?

8. Did you find sanctuary in books, art, nature or faith growing up? What did that refuge teach you or provide?

9. Did you grow up in a household struggling with addiction, mental health challenges, incarceration, or abuse? How did you develop resilience to overcome this environment?

10. When did you first feel like you belonged? What gave you that reassuring sense of connection?

The stories within you are the key to outstanding essays. Here are some examples:

"Moving schools each year due to my dad's military service showed me how to adapt and connect anywhere."

"Caring for my brother with autism taught me empathy and nurturing for those who think differently."

"Translating for my immigrant parents as a child gave me a sense of purpose and an appreciation for languages."

GET STELLAR RECOMMENDATION LETTERS

The key to stellar recommendation letters is threefold:

1. Ask for letters of recommendation early.
2. Ask only those professors and mentors who are big fans of yours.
3. Make it super easy for those mentors.

Flag for your mentors in the summer that you'll be asking for letters of recommendation the following semester. Let them know six to eight weeks in advance once you have the specific list of schools and each school's deadline.

I asked four professors and one internship supervisor if they were willing to send out recommendation letters, clarifying my intention to apply to over *fifteen* universities. Luckily, the recommender can usually reuse the same recommendation letter. All happily agreed to send recommendation letters, except one, who said they were too busy to handle recommendation letters that semester.

Refer to the advice in Chapter 6 to ensure professors are excited about you before you ask.

To make writing letters of recommendation easy, send your professors and mentors a curated list of three to six accomplishments you'd love for them to highlight. This saves them the time of having to come up with specific accomplishments of yours, *and* it ensures that each of your letters of recommendation highlights a different set of accomplishments. In the same email, also send your professors your comprehensive list of accomplishments in case they don't love the three to six accomplishments you chose, as well as a one-page résumé (the same one that you're sending to the school to which they will write) and transcripts. Avoid making your professors send an unnecessary email asking for these documents.

Sample email:

Dear [Professor/mentor's name],

I hope you are doing great. I am currently starting to apply to four-year universities, and I am in need of a few letters of recommendation. As I mentioned earlier [you can include here when this was, with specifics that the professor will remember], I would be honored if you could write a letter of recommendation for me.

To make the process as easy as possible for you, I have compiled a list of three to six accomplishments that I would love for you to highlight in your letter. These specific accomplishments represent some of my proudest moments, and I believe they would help to showcase my skills and abilities.
[Insert three to six specific accomplishments here]
I have also attached a comprehensive list of all my accomplishments in case you prefer to highlight other achievements instead.

Thank you so much for your time and support throughout my academic journey. I am truly grateful for your guidance and mentorship. Please let me know if there is anything else I can provide to make this process easier for you.

Best regards,
[Your Name]

Regrettably, universities don't seem to value letters of recommendation from jobs like hourly food industry or retail work. I once got pretty much a *perfect* score as a server from an undercover restaurant reviewer. My employer was thrilled. Experiences like this, even if written in a glowing recommendation from a restaurant manager, aren't impressive to universities. I wouldn't seek letters of recommendation from your hourly wage employers unless your part-time work is very relevant to your major, is considered "professional" or white collar, or is very unusual.

SAY NO TO COSTLY ERRORS

- Make a system to *never* miss a deadline.
    - Some schools have earlier deadlines for financial aid consideration or transfer students. Update your college application-tracking spreadsheet regularly and check it weekly. Make sure the deadlines are easily visible. If you find that you don't review the spreadsheet regularly enough, add the deadlines to your Google Calendar with two-day, one-week, and three-week reminders.

- Check for transfer student eligibility.
    - A school might only promise to meet full financial need for incoming freshmen, not transfer students. Call to confirm if the website doesn't clearly state transfers are eligible.

- Double-check each university's application instructions.
    - Ensure that you have submitted every single essay they request. Some schools have additional instructions, like sending letters of recommendation directly to them rather than uploading them.

- Keep track of the requirements.
    - Avoid any surprises, e.g. certain schools require additional essays. Spend fifteen to twenty minutes on each college website's application requirements; call the university to clarify further if needed.

- Proofread your essay.

    - I had a careless typo in my Harvard essay. I'll never know if that contributed to me not getting in. I should have proofread the essay more closely. Have many people proofread your essay.

- Have a backup plan.

    - Make sure at least two of your schools have acceptance rates of around 30 percent (or higher), as "**safety schools**." If you're still very worried or weren't able to fully implement the plan above for any reason, also apply to a nearby public university. Some public universities offer generous financial aid guarantees, but only for students from the nearby community—so this would be an ideal backup. Given that your college résumé is competitive enough to consider top universities, you're very likely to get merit-based scholarships at your local public universities.

COMPARE FINANCIAL AID PACKAGES AND ASK FOR MORE AID

When you're looking at financial aid packages, focus on how much you'll have to pay directly to the university. Universities tend to include extra costs (like phone bills, textbooks, travel, and miscellaneous) in their estimated total cost, meaning your financial aid package is aiming to ensure you also have ample pocket money. I find that the extra indirect costs estimates tend to be high, especially since meals are included in room and board. Calculate how much you actually have to pay the university. That's what you'll have to pay up front by the beginning of the semester.

If your expected family contribution according to the CSS Profile and FAFSA is $0, most likely your financial aid will fully cover your tuition but will still include a $3,500 subsidized loan plus on-campus work and potentially some small parent/student contribution. Government-subsidized loans *do not* accrue interest while you are in school, and they are the cheapest student loans available.

If your expected family contribution according to the financial aid assessments is higher than the FAFSA-calculated family contribution, your expected parent/student contribution will be higher.

Different schools calculate financial need differently, so I recommend waiting to commit to a university until you hear back with several schools' financial aid packages.

If the schools calculate that your expected family contribution is higher than what your family can afford, and you're expecting to need to take out additional loans:

1. Call the school to ask if they can boost your scholarship offer, citing hardship and any extenuating circumstances that might not have been fully covered in the financial aid assessments. If you live near the school, go in person to the financial aid and scholarship offices.
2. Mention other schools' more competitive scholarship packages, especially if you received merit-based scholarships at other universities.
3. Ask if you can be considered for any additional funding sources.

If you find that you do need loans separate from government-subsidized loans to cover what you pay to the school, you have several months to fill this gap (refer to Chapter 2 for more detailed ways to fill this gap). If you're not able to fill this gap, only take government unsubsidized loans.

Types of loans:

- **Direct Subsidized Loans** are federal loans based on financial need.
- **Direct Unsubsidized Loans** are based on the cost of attendance and other financial aid received.

- **Direct PLUS Loans** are credit-based and unsubsidized loans for parents and graduate/professional students.

- **Private student loans** are issued by banks, other financial institutions, or sometimes even schools. These often have costlier interest rates, require a cosigner, good credit score, and payments while in school.

Do **not** consider a private loan, even if you are offered a competitive interest rate. Government loans (subsidized or unsubsidized) are the only loans that qualify for *government loan forgiveness programs*. Government loans also qualify for other perks, including no payments necessary while the recipient is in school, fixed interest rates, income-driven repayment plans, temporary postponement of payments, no prepayment penalty fees, and forgiveness after doing public service.

Private loans typically cannot match the perks of government direct loans. Even if the interest rate for a private loan might appear lower, the fact that the interest rate is *variable* means the private loan can become significantly more expensive later.

Overall, you can expect to be offered up to the amounts listed below in government loans.

Undergraduate Federal Student Loan Limits

Year	Dependent total amount	Independent total amount
First year	$5,500 ($3,500 subsidized, $2,000 unsubsidized)	$9,500 ($3,500 subsidized, $6,000 unsubsidized)
Second year	$6,500 ($4,500 subsidized, $2,000 unsubsidized)	$10,500 ($4,500 subsidized, $6,000 unsubsidized)
Third year and beyond	$7,500 ($5,500 subsidized, $2,000 unsubsidized)	$12,500 ($5,500 subsidized, $7,000 unsubsidized)

Source: https://www.forbes.com/advisor/student-loans/student-loan-limits/.

CHAPTER 9
MAINTAIN YOUR MOMENTUM

KEYS TO REACHING YOUR
POST-COLLEGE GOALS AND DREAMS

By this point, you will hopefully be accepted at a university that has promised you a full ride (or nearly full ride) because of your income level.

Apart from a massive scholarship, you should also have some *great study habits*, *weekly and daily routines*, and *excellent productivity*. Now that you don't have to worry about expensive car repairs and gas money—since dorms are within walking distance from class—and food costs (thanks to the meal plan!), you should have a lot more time to enjoy being a student.

You worked hard for this, and I hope you enjoy the benefits of that. Now is the time to keep in mind that your continued hard work can continue to pay off in the future.

Your **college résumé** that helped you get into top universities can also help you get top fellowships and scholarships for graduate school, and even dream jobs.

To keep being a competitive student for this, I'd recommend keeping your college résumé competitive by:

- Ensuring every single summer has one professional internship.
- Working at an on-campus job (or two jobs) to cover your expenses.
- Having one on-campus leadership position.
- Volunteering at one place.

Roughly every two weeks, I would apply to **national fellowships or scholarships** that were related to my major. My professors flagged opportunities for me because I was open about my eagerness to find graduate school funding.

Some students, after the grueling process of applying to top schools, feel burned out and "coast" at university. If this is what you want to do, that's fine too. I'd recommend (at minimum) ensuring you get a professional internship or other academic, research, or professional experience every summer because these are valuable for getting post-college jobs and keeping you in the running for generous fellowships and scholarships. Focus your class essay and research assignments on important topics, so that these can double as powerful, relevant writing samples for job applications.

GETTING YOUR DREAM CAREER / POST-COLLEGE PLANS

According to Pew Research, *college-educated households headed by college-educated individuals whose parents had a college degree earn an average of $135,000 annually*, compared with those headed by college-educated individuals whose parents did not have a college degree, who earn an average of $99,600 yearly. Whether a parent has a college degree impacts their children's future earnings, even after their children move out and become heads of households themselves.

Low-income and first-generation students can combat this huge pay gap by planning for their post-graduation life throughout college. A lot of students end up not thinking about their post-college plans until their senior year of college. Don't be one of these students, especially if your family doesn't consist of college graduates or professional career-holders who can guide you through the process of getting professional entry-level jobs or reviewing graduate schools.

Along with getting great professional experience and having a mentality that seeks to test out different careers from your first year at college, I recommend setting aside time each week (at the very latest, by your junior year) to focus on a post-college strategy and actions stemming from that strategy.

My recommended strategy for preparing for post-college:

Don't get obsessed with analyzing longer-term plans—many successful people didn't predict where they'd end up; the world will change, and you will change. The aim is simply to have some hypotheses in mind, which you'll "test" with your next job.

Take on an **"optimizing"** strategy as you review careers based on your own values and goals and the types of skills and experiences you want to have. For example, if you're primarily motivated by impactful careers, analyze the impact of a career opportunity in terms of

- How pressing the problem is that you'd work on

- How much of a contribution you could make in tackling the problem

- Your personal fit with the opportunity, which depends on your abilities and "career capital" (skills, connections, and reputation)

Be aware that there are various indirect paths to making change, such as communicating ideas, conducting research, or donating to effective organizations, which can often be just as (or even more) effective than working at a charity.

For high-level strategic guidance on choosing a career, I recommend my favorite career guidebook, *80,000 Hours: Find a Fulfilling Career That Does Good*. You can get it as an e-book on Amazon for $4, paperback for about $15, or get it for free by signing up for the *80,000 Hours* newsletter via this link: https://80000hours.org/book. This is the book that I read after graduating from college, and it helped me decide what kind of career I wanted to pursue.

YOUR ACTION PLAN FOR EXCITING CAREER PATHS

Generate a long list of options—most people consider too few. It's hard to visualize the sheer number and variety of cool companies, nonprofits, and government jobs there are. When I unexpectedly got laid off from a nonprofit role, I generated a very long list of options.

The first step is to build a spreadsheet of very specific jobs and educational opportunities (like fellowships or grad programs) to pursue. To generate more options, work backward from your longer-term goals by reviewing the careers and résumés of people whose career paths you admire. You can also work forward by looking for exciting job opportunities listed on job websites now.

Getting a clear sense of what types of roles you like, *and what those roles require,* is key to getting them.

Your goal is to apply to *lots* of interesting jobs and professional opportunities (like fellowships) each week.

I recommend setting up a weekly routine of generating ideas, applying to jobs/fellowships, and doing targeted networking. Perhaps replace the weekend time slot that you dedicated to university/scholarship searches with these steps before, during, after, or instead of the 80,000 Hours career planning course. Below is a step-by-step process to do weekly to generate opportunities.

1. Check out LinkedIn, Idealist, the 80,000 Hours job board, the 80,000 Hours list of career reviews, Monster, and career newsletters that focus on your topic(s) of interest for job openings and ideas. Check back for new job roles regularly.

2. Apply to any new job openings you come across. Make sure you pull from your very detailed long résumé to draft a one-page résumé tailored to that job. Keep each résumé version and documents you used to apply to each role in a "Résumés/Job Search" document for quickly reusing for similar roles.

3. In a spreadsheet, keep track of cool jobs and internship roles you are excited about, even if these roles are too senior for you now or you don't meet the qualifications. These roles can serve as your "guiding stars"—you can model your career on the people with these roles now. Find the people who have these roles on LinkedIn and

check out what roles they held before they landed your dream roles. Use these roles to generate new types of roles to consider and apply for.

4. Also add any educational opportunities or fellowships (regardless of whether you currently qualify), noting their relevant deadlines. Add these to your spreadsheet to remember to apply when you do qualify.

Once you've applied to new relevant job openings, work on finding out more about other employers in that industry. Consider reaching out to early-career people in that field for fifteen-minute phone calls for more detailed information about the field or employer, the type of information you can't google. This serves to both grow your network in the field *and* help you build a more accurate map of which employers are excellent to work for and which might be worth avoiding. You also might be able to ask this person for a reference or referral if there is a job opening later and you made a good impression. The employee often has an incentive to give referrals. Many companies offer employees thousand-dollar bonuses for referrals that get hired.

5. In another tab in that spreadsheet, compile a list of employers that tend to have those job roles. To find these, search on the same websites as above, but this time search using the job position as your keyword. Also, search using different but similar names for that job position. These are employers who might have openings in the future or would be very interested in your niche. You'll want to know who the main players are in this topic or industry and start developing some contacts there.

6. Start a third tab in the spreadsheet. Compile a list of contacts who work or have worked at these employers and are your first- or second-degree contacts. A first-degree LinkedIn connection is someone to whom you are directly connected on the platform—you have accepted each other's connection request. A second-degree connection is someone who is connected to one of your first-degree

connections, but not to you. LinkedIn makes it easy to find these contacts. Search for the name of the employer on LinkedIn. If you don't get good results with that, narrow your results even further by clicking "People."

7. You might not have many first- or second-degree contacts yet because you're just starting out in your career and on LinkedIn. Search through the list of people associated with your favorite employers for any people who you might be able to cold email. I recommend focusing only on people who (1) are alumni of your school; (2) are from the same city or region as you; (3) are entry-level and so might be more likely to talk to students; and (4) have some other similarity to you (e.g., they were a community college student who focused on topics you've focused on).

8. Write them a *highly* personalized message, highlighting what you have in common, whom you know in common, and why you're interested in knowing more about their specific career trajectory or experience in their specific niche. If your weekly job search routine is on a weekend, schedule the email to be sent out on Monday and ask for a fifteen- to twenty-minute call on Thursday or Friday afternoon (*use their time zone, not yours*).

    a. Do **not** ever ask these contacts for a job. Prepare questions that are personalized for them: How did they develop this niche? How does this employer compare to the others in their niche? What specific gap is this employer focusing on? What are the books, blogs, career newsletters, or professional online Facebook or LinkedIn groups this contact has been reading that are most influential?

    b. You can message them on LinkedIn using Premium or by finding their email online, possibly from their reports or presentations.

    c. I highly recommend Ramit Sethi's articles on how to make information interviews efficient and useful for both you and the contact: https://www.iwillteachyoutoberich.com/blog/informational-interview-ques-tions-that-create-a-lasting-impression/.

9. Read the books, blogs, or articles and/or join the on-line professional group(s) that the contacts recommend. Thank them. If you find something useful to their niche, periodically send it to them to keep in touch.

CONSIDER NICHE OPPORTUNITIES TO LAUNCH YOUR POST-COLLEGE CAREER

Here are some examples of post-college opportunities, my favorite being fellowships. Fellowships are scholarships, grants, or other types of support like fixed-term employment and mentorship given to individuals to support a particular field of study, research project, or professional development. These awards may be offered by universities, government agencies, foundations, or corporations. The award money is usually used to cover the cost of tuition, living expenses, and other associated costs.

You can find early-career fellowships by using the same tactics you used to find scholarships: review scholarship/fellowship websites, ask guidance counselors, ask your department/academic major heads, and ask your professors. I also recommend signing up for career guidance and academic department notices at other top universities. Often, you don't even have to be a student at the university in question in order to sign up.

Here are some fellowships to get you thinking. For most of these, I personally know someone who won one and can assure you that they are normal people, like you and me! If you've followed the steps in this book, you are a competitive recent grad.

- **Treasury International Affairs Fellowship:** A two-year program for new college graduates to help shape international economic policy for the United States at the Treasury Department.

- **Pickering and Rangel Fellowships:** These offer nearly full funding for a master's program, and include two paid summer internships (one of which is abroad). These include a five-year Foreign Service commitment.

- **Truman Scholar Program:** This provides graduate students with leadership and public service opportunities. Fellows receive a stipend, travel expenses, and access to professional development and mentorship.

- **Fulbright:** This program provides international exchange for students, scholars, and professionals to study and teach in over 140 countries. It includes funding for research, study, and teaching.

- **Rhodes Scholarship:** This scholarship program is one of the oldest and most prestigious scholarships and provides funding for study at the University of Oxford in England for up to three years of study in any field of study.

- **Marshall Scholarship:** This scholarship provides funding for study at any university in the United Kingdom. It includes a living stipend and tuition for two years of study.

- **Schwarzman Scholars:** This program funds study at Tsinghua University in China. It includes a stipend and tuition for one year of study in the Schwarzman College of Computing, Business, Global Affairs, or International Studies.

- **Gates Cambridge Scholarship:** This fully funds two years of graduate school at the University of Cambridge in England, in any field of study.

- **Boren Scholarships and Fellowships:** These fund U.S. citizens studying less commonly taught languages in critical world regions. Open to undergraduates and graduates in accredited U.S. programs, funds cover program costs and predeparture language study. Recipients receive advising, career support, and federal agency employment resources. Award amounts range from $8,000 (summer

STEM) to $20,000 (full-year undergrad) or $30,000 (full-year graduate).

- **NSF Graduate Research Fellowship Program:** This program provides research funding for graduate students in STEM fields. It includes a stipend and tuition for up to three years of study.

- **Aspire Leaders Program:** This program supports students from disadvantaged backgrounds, providing access to fully funded HarvardX courses, live seminars with Harvard faculty, global peer collaboration, and grants/mentorship opportunities.

- Specific for community college or transfer students:

  - **Community College Global Affairs Fellowship:** This free summer program, geared for community college, transfer, and non-traditional students interested in global affairs, offers a two-week enrichment program in Washington, D.C., and a two-month, virtual, one-on-one mentorship. Apply at https://www.meridian.org/.

For community college transfers: Often community college transfer students miss out on these opportunities. For example, the world-famous Rhodes Scholarship requires *eight* letters of recommendation. Application preparation should typically start the summer before senior year of college. Most community college students transfer in junior year and struggle to (1) find out about prestigious opportunities in time; (2) develop relationships with professors for letters of recommendation; and (3) take enough university classes (or hold prestigious positions) to qualify. I recommend you look into prestigious scholarships and fellowships as soon as you know you have been admitted to a university. You can even call the university's scholarship office before they're officially in classes, to start preparing. Ideally, you could use the university's resources to find a prestigious internship or research opportunity the summer before your first semester (junior year) at the new university.

YOU GOT THIS!

I hope that you have learned that you can shoot for generous selective universities, regardless of your background. I also hope that you have gained the confidence to pursue these opportunities, even if you don't have the guidance of a professional network yet. But above all, I want to leave you with the message that the most important aspect of this is that you learn how much you're capable of.

You may have been conditioned to believe that your opportunities are limited. It's easy to feel discouraged, especially when you lack the guidance and support that your wealthier peers may have. I know you are capable of achieving great things. The more you believe in yourself and your abilities, the more opportunities will open up to you.

Apart from getting into college, you will make a profound impact by investing in your personal growth and your goals. You're crafting a study system that works for you, setting achievable goals, and celebrating your successes along the way. By confronting and shedding limiting beliefs, these will no longer hold you back in life.

The journey to college can be difficult, but the destination is not the only thing that matters. Every step you take toward your goals is an opportunity to strengthen your faith in yourself. Throughout this process, I encourage you to be kind to yourself, to trust your instincts, and to remember that you are worthy of every opportunity that comes your way.

Finally, I want to acknowledge the challenges that you will face as a lower-income student entering these competitive programs. The road ahead is not easy, but I believe in you. I believe that you have the strength and resilience to overcome any obstacle and that you will emerge from this process stronger and more confident than ever before. And I hope that when you do, you will look back on this book and pass it along to another student who will follow in your pioneering footsteps.

MAKE MY DAY: SPREAD THE WORD

If you enjoyed *The Underdog's Guide to Scholarships*, would you mind taking a minute to write a review on Amazon? Even a short review helps, and it would mean a lot to me.

If someone you care about is dreaming about university but struggling to get there, please send them a copy of this book. Whether you decide to gift it on Amazon or pass along a PDF, it warms my heart either way.

If you'd like to get free bonus materials from the book and receive updates on my future projects, sign up for my newsletter at abiolvera.com.

ACKNOWLEDGMENTS

Profound thanks to Marjorie Riche, Katlyn Batuigas, Monica Markowski, Lynette Bye, Morgan Livingston, and Alexandra Roberts for reviewing early pages and sharing your insightful journeys. You strengthened this work immensely. Also, a loving thanks to Alex Long who was a critical source of support throughout every stage of the book, helping me brainstorm through the bumps in the road, tirelessly providing feedback and review. Amber Qureshi, my editor, thank you for going above and beyond, championing this book and its mission. George Hiller, thank you for your thoughtful suggestions and your dedication to nuestras comunidades. Jeff Maxim, Damon Sasi, Richie Dominguez, Elena Madrid, Dr. Manuel Montoya, Dr. Stephen Long, Amanda DeMundrun, Lionel Palma, Beth Chancy, Nick Minnix, Fred Haiman, and Bella Forristal: thanks so much for your uplifting feedback in the early stages of the book. Charumati Haran, thank you for your meticulous review and support.

My gratitude to Semnitz for the cover design, HMDPublishing for formatting, and Michael McConnell for copyediting. Sincere thanks also to the high schoolers and recent grads who beta-read this book. I am also very grateful for the Center of Effective Altruism grant which supported the finalizing and early distribution of this book.

To all those who shared your stories of triumph and obstacles for this book, my heartfelt thanks. You are why I pursued this project – to guide the path for those following you.

APPENDIX

APPENDIX A

SEVENTY-FIVE UNIVERSITIES OFFERING TO MEET FULL FINANCIAL NEED

Of the 4,000-odd colleges and universities across the country, these are the only ones that you need to consider. These promises can change. For the most updated list of these seventy-five, check out: https://money.com/colleges-that-meet-full-financial-need/.

Amherst College
Barnard College
Bates College
Babson College*
Boston College
Bowdoin College
Brown University
Bryn Mawr College
California Institute of Technology
Carleton College
Case Western Reserve University*
Claremont McKenna College
Colby College
Colgate University
College of the Holy Cross
Colorado College
Columbia University
Connecticut College
Cornell University
Dartmouth College
Davidson College
Denison University*
Dickinson College*

Duke University
Emory University
Franklin & Marshall College
Franklin W. Olin College of Engineering
Georgetown University
Grinnell College
Hamilton College
Harvard University
Harvey Mudd College
Haverford College
Johns Hopkins University
Kenyon College
Lafayette College
Macalester College
Marietta College*
Massachusetts Institute of Technology
Middlebury College
Mount Holyoke College
Northeastern University*
Oberlin College
Occidental College
Pitzer College

Pomona College
Princeton University
Reed College
Rice University
Scripps College
Skidmore College*
Smith College
Stanford University
St. Olaf College*
Swarthmore College
Thomas Aquinas College
Trinity College
Tufts University*
Union College
University of Chicago
University of North Carolina at Chapel Hill

University of Notre Dame
University of Pennsylvania
University of Richmond
University of Southern California
University of Virginia
Vanderbilt University
Vassar College
Wake Forest University
Washington and Lee University
Washington University in St. Louis
Wellesley College
Wesleyan University
Williams College
Yale University

According to Money.com and Peterson's, the eleven colleges with asterisks report meeting 100 percent of financial need for freshmen, but for not all undergraduates (i.e., the promise might not extend to transfer students).

APPENDIX B

COLLEGES PROMISING NO LOANS IN THEIR FINANCIAL AID PACKAGE

A subset of those seventy-five promise to not include loans in their financial package. According to LendingTree.com, twenty-one universities are "full need met" with a no-loans policy for *all* students, an additional fifteen offer the no-loan promise to low-income students, and an additional eighteen universities across various states offer no-loan promises to in-state students.

No-loans colleges for all students:

1. Amherst College
2. Berea College
3. Bowdoin College
4. Brown University
5. Colby College
6. College of the Ozarks
7. Columbia University
8. Davidson College
9. Grinnell College
10. Harvard University
11. Johns Hopkins University (need-blind, 7.5 percent acceptance rate)
12. Northwestern University
13. Pomona College
14. Princeton University
15. Stanford University
16. Swarthmore College

17. University of Chicago
18. University of Pennsylvania
19. Vanderbilt University
20. Washington and Lee University
21. Yale University

No-loans colleges for low-income students:

1. Colgate University: No-loan initiative applies to students with family incomes below $175,000.

2. Connecticut College: If your family's income falls below a certain threshold, your financial aid package will reduce or eliminate student loans. Contact the school for more details.

3. Cornell University: Families who earn under $60,000 with typical assets for this income range aren't expected to contribute toward tuition and therefore won't be offered any loans.

4. Dartmouth College: The Dartmouth Scholarship will cover full tuition if your family's income is $125,000 or less with typical assets.

5. Duke University: You can attend loan-free if your family earns under $40,000.

6. Emory University: If you're an undergraduate student and you qualify for need-based aid, you'll automatically enter the expanded Emory Advantage program. This program helps students graduate debt-free.

7. Haverford College: Students whose families have incomes below $60,000 won't have loans offered in their financial aid packages.

8. Lafayette College: Dedicated to lowering or eliminating student loan debt for students with incomes below $150,000.

9. Miami University (Ohio): Miami Access Fellows awards grants and scholarships for students with incomes less than $35,000.

10. Michigan State University: The Spartan Advantage Program will cover your full-time tuition, room and board, books, and course materials if your family's income is at or below the federal poverty level.

11. Rice University: The Rice Investment program offers full tuition, fees and room and board scholarships to undergraduates with incomes of $75,000 or less. Students whose families make between $75,000 and $140,000 can receive a full-tuition scholarship, and those earning between $140,000 and $200,000 are eligible for half-price tuition.

12. Tufts University: Students with family incomes at or below $60,000 typically receive a no-loans financial aid package.

13. University of North Carolina at Chapel Hill: The Carolina Covenant is an aid program that helps families at or below 200 percent of the poverty level. If eligible, the university will help you graduate debt-free.

14. Washington University in St. Louis: No-loans packages are available for families earning $75,000 or less a year.

15. Wellesley College: Wellesley recently expanded its $0-Loan group to include students whose families have a household income of less than $100,000.

16. Wesleyan University: The no-loans policy is available to US citizens, permanent residents, undocumented students, and DACA students with family incomes of $120,000 or less. Typical assets must be $400,000 or less.

No-loans colleges for in-state students:

Arizona

1. Arizona State University: The ASU College Attainment Grant Program, President Barack Obama Program and

Arizona Promise Program cover tuition and fees for up to four years for Arizona students eligible to receive a Pell Grant.

2. University of Arizona: The Arizona Assurance Grant offers up to $10,000 per academic year for four years. Students must have a family income of $27,000 or less, have an EFC of $0, and be eligible for a Pell Grant.

California

3. University of California schools: Residents who qualify for financial aid with a family income below $80,000 won't need to pay system-wide tuition or fees.

Connecticut

4. Fairfield University: The Bridgeport Tuition Grant is offered to high school graduates from Bridgeport, Conn., with a household income below $50,000 and typical assets for this income range.

Georgia

5. Georgia Institute of Technology: The G. Wayne Clough Georgia Tech Promise Scholarship helps in-state students with income below $33,300 obtain a debt-free degree from Georgia Tech.

Illinois

6. University of Illinois at Urbana-Champaign: The Illinois Commitment covers up to four years of tuition and fees for qualified in-state students if their family's income is $67,100 or less. Family assets must be $50,000 or less.

Indiana

7. Indiana University: Indiana residents must sign the Scholar Pledge in seventh or eighth grade, graduate with a GPA of 2.5 or higher, and meet the income threshold to qualify for the Indiana University Bloomington (IUB) 21st Centu-

ry Scholarship Program. If accepted, the school will cover 100 percent of your tuition and mandatory fees.

Kentucky

8. University of Louisville: Residents with a household income at or below 150 percent of the poverty threshold are eligible to apply for the Cardinal Covenant, which helps students graduate debt-free from an undergraduate program.

Michigan

9. University of Michigan: U-M's Go Blue Guarantee will pay tuition and mandatory fees for up to four years for residents pursuing their first bachelor's degree if their family's income is $65,000 or less, with assets below $50,000. You can still receive some tuition support even if you earn more.

North Carolina

10. Appalachian State University: The Murray Family ACCESS Program helps low-income North Carolina students graduate debt-free. To qualify, you must attend school full time with a household income at or below 100 percent of the federal poverty threshold, plus an EFC of $0 after filing your FAFSA.

Tennessee

11. Bryan College: Residents with a household income of up to $36,000 pursuing their first bachelor's degree can apply for the Bryan Opportunity Scholarship Program. This renewable award can cover up to the full amount for tuition, fees, and room and board.

12. University of Tennessee: The UT Promise Scholarship covers the remaining cost of tuition and mandatory fees after federal, state, and institutional aid. Students need a family income below $60,000 and must qualify for the HOPE Scholarship.

Texas

13. Texas State University: The Bobcat Promise allows first-year students the opportunity to attend tuition-free if their family's income falls below $50,000.

14. Lamar University: The Lamar Promise Program covers in-state tuition and fees (but not room and board) for undergraduate Texas residents if their household income doesn't exceed $40,000.

15. University of Texas at El Paso: The Paydirt Promise program will pay your full tuition and mandatory fees if your household income is $75,000 or less.

16. University of Texas at Dallas: The Tuition Promise program will cover any remaining tuition expenses after federal, state, and institutional funds if your family's income is $65,000 or less.

17. Texas A&M University: The Aggie Assurance provides full tuition support for students with a family income of $60,000 or less.

Vermont

18. University of Vermont: The UVM Promise helps low-income students attend tuition-free. To qualify, your family income must be $60,000 or less.

Virginia

19. College of William and Mary: Starting in the 2023–2024 school year, William and Mary will provide scholarship aid to cover tuition and fees for all in-state undergraduates who are Pell Grant eligible.

These promises can change. Check directly at the Lending-Tree website and each university's website for the latest data: https://www.lendingtree.com/student/colleges-no-student-loans-policy/

APPENDIX C

Below are examples of neglected research questions you could focus on within the field of existential risk—that is, research and advocacy aimed at reducing the chances of a human-imperiling catastrophe.

Engineered Pandemics

- Run scenario-planning exercises for severe engineered pandemics.

Asteroids and Comets

- Research the deflection of 1 km+ asteroids and comets.
- Improve understanding of what could happen if a small asteroid hits Earth, causing a "volcanic winter" effect because of dust and debris blocking out sunlight.

Nuclear Weapons

- Investigate which parts of the world appear most robust to the effects of nuclear winter and how likely civilization is to be able to survive there.

Climate

- Explore the concept of the runaway greenhouse effect, which refers to a scenario where increased greenhouse gas concentrations lead to a self-perpetuating cycle of rising temperatures. Are there any ways this could be more likely than is currently understood? Are there any ways we could decisively rule this risk out?
- Improve our understanding of extreme warming (e.g., 5–20 °C), including searching for concrete mechanisms

through which warming could pose a plausible threat of human extinction or the global collapse of civilization.

Environmental Damage

- Improve our understanding of whether any kind of resource depletion currently poses an existential risk.

- Improve our understanding of current biodiversity loss (both regional and global) and how it compares with that of past extinction events.

General

- Identify the most significant factors that pose a risk to the survival of human civilization. Consider both the magnitude of these risks and the effectiveness of potential measures to reduce them.

- Target efforts at reducing the likelihood of military conflicts between the US, Russia, and China.

- Investigate food substitutes in case of an extreme and lasting reduction in the world's ability to supply food.

- Improve our understanding of the chance that civilization will recover after a global collapse, what might prevent this, and how to improve the odds.

Source: https://80000hours.org/2020/04/long-termist-policy-ideas/.

If you already have a topic of interest, you can check out 80,000 Hours' research questions for each discipline, ranging from biology to philosophy to law to psychology, etc.

https://80000hours.org/articles/research-questions-by-discipline/

APPENDIX D

EXAMPLE OF A SUCCESSFUL ESSAY

As an example of a successful essay, below is one of Lynette Bye's two Harvard admissions essays. Note that she's not just rehashing her résumé. She's adding color and an emotional story behind one of her résumé feats.

Dark shadows lurked around the king size bed where I lay. My cousin's guest room harbored no threats, but, as a six-year-old, it frightened me to fall asleep alone in the strange space. Not until my Grandpa Henry died from leukemia a year later did I really understood how dangerous the cancer was that my mom battled, or why my dad had sent us kids away—so he could stay with her while she underwent surgery. I then comprehended clearly the foe of cancer but was powerless to help either of my loved ones.

Ten years later, my pastor announced that our church was forming a Relay for Life team to fight cancer. The team needed a captain. I immediately wondered if they would let a teenager captain the team. Over the next week, I consulted my parents and a previous captain to see if I was up to the challenge. Ultimately, I plunged in. As my sister reasoned, "How hard can it be leading people around a track?"

The Warm Beach Cancer Killers were born, and recruitment started. Every Sunday, I unfolded my table, talking with people, handing out registration forms, and holding meetings. Recruiting succeeded so well that we almost doubled the sixteen-person team limit. Team members ranged from twelve years old to eighty. My sister stepped up as an official captain for a second team, though all twenty-eight volunteers functioned as one team.

I had thought my biggest challenge would be recruiting team members. I soon learned that motivating them to participate required more than just getting them signed up. I called each team member with details of the first team fundraiser. Only six people showed up. The six of us canvassed town cajoling local businesses into buying advertising time at the Relay. I photoshopped the business names into colorful signs stamped in purple "Supports Relay for Life" to hang on walker's backs. My small but mighty band collected over four hundred dollars that afternoon, succeeding beyond expectations.

The day of the event dawned. I arrived at the track early and didn't leave until a chaotic twenty-four hours later. I charted schedules so that walkers always represented our teams on the track. I managed our onsite fundraisers of cookies and necklaces. I led our group activities, even rapping in the Relay Idol competition. I cheered my team as the night wore on and their feet slowed. It was a complete success. Not only did the team members love it, but we proudly raised three thousand and two dollars.

I discovered my ability to fight back against cancer, and I brought others along to make a difference one person could not make alone. I learned that leadership takes effort, enthusiasm, and a willingness to invest more than one expects anyone else to contribute. I set out to recruit a team and raise fifteen hundred dollars. I finished with two teams and three thousand dollars raised, and I grew as a leader.

ADDITIONAL USEFUL RESOURCES

Books on strategy:

1. *How to Win at College: Surprising Secrets for Success from the Country's Top Students*, by Cal Newport.

2. *How to Become a Straight-A Student: The Unconventional Strategies Real College Students Use to Score High While Studying Less*, by Cal Newport.

3. *How to Be a High School Superstar: A Revolutionary Plan to Get into College by Standing Out (Without Burning Out)*, by Cal Newport (Lynette Bye's favorite Newport book on this topic).

4. *The Scholarship System: 6 Simple Steps on How to Win Scholarships and Financial Aid*, by Jocelyn Paonita.

5. *Find a Fulfilling Career That Does Good by 80,000 Hours.* You can buy this on Amazon or get it for free by signing up for the *80,000 Hours* newsletter via this link: https://80000hours.org/book

Websites:

1. LendingTree's continually updated list of no-loans colleges.

https://www.lendingtree.com/student/colleges-no-student-loans-policy

2. List of seventy-five colleges that meet full financial need, although these schools might include loans as part of your financial aid package.

https://money.com/colleges-that-meet-full-financial-need

3. Lynette Bye's productivity and career coaching blog.

https://lynettebye.com/blog

4. 80,000 Hours' research-backed career advice, neglected research opportunities, and social impact strategies.

https://80000hours.org

5. 80,000 Hours: "What Are the World's Most Pressing Problems?"

https://80000hours.org/problem-profiles

6. My favorite article on how to email busy people.

https://www.iwillteachyoutoberich.com/blog/how-to-connect-with-busy-people

7. 80,000 Hours' high-impact research questions for various disciplines, ranging from biology to philosophy to law to psychology.

https://80000hours.org/articles/research-questions-by-discipline

8. Questbridge's website provides grade-specific checklists, tips for choosing high school classes preparing for standardized tests, and planning your summers.

https://www.questbridge.org

9. "SAT / ACT Prep, Grades, and College Admissions Strategies Online Guides and Tips"

https://blog.prepscholar.com

Some summer programs and internships ideas:

1. National Parks' youth and young adults programs for people between the ages of fifteen and thirty.

https://www.nps.gov/subjects/youthprograms/jobs-and-internships.htm

2. Smithsonian Institution large summer internship program in a variety of fields.

https://internships.si.edu